Acclaim for **VIDAS**: *Deep in Mexico and Spain*

"Highly sensitive to the transformations of our planet, Edward Stanton is also aware of the evolutions in travel writing: while in the last century it focused on distant places, some of them missing on our maps, in our time it centers around people. This author, wise without being pedantic, playful yet profound, invites us to embark on a great adventure: to celebrate the glorious diversity of our worlds, embodied in the persons we find each day and everywhere."

—Alberto Ruy Sánchez, Founder, *Artes de México,*
Winner 2017 National Prize for Literature

"An engaging coming-of-age account that explores manhood across cultural boundaries . . . The author is a lyrical writer . . . Descriptions of his participation in iconic events, such as the running of the bulls or his first bullfight, are elegant and stand up to the inevitable comparisons to Steinbeck and Hemingway . . . An enjoyable reading experience."

—*Kirkus Reviews*

"Edward Stanton's youthful heart evokes the cherished moments of discovering, exploring and returning again and again to Mexico and Spain. Unique and stirring memories that evoke the power of friendship, language, legends, foods and wines, ways of life and death, the past, a vibrant present. Through many voices, lyrical prose, a chorus of Spanish *jotas* and *romances*, Mexican *boleros* and *rancheras*, the writer has composed a passionate song that resonates across an ocean, two countries and continents."

—Ana Merino, Winner 2020 Premio Nadal,
Spain's Premier Award for Novel

Praise for Other Books by Edward Stanton

Road of Stars to Santiago

"Edward Stanton recounts his adventures with stylish conviction."

—James Michener (Pulitzer Prize for Literature)

"This book could become a source for understanding our troubled times."

—William Watson, M.I.T.

Hemingway and Spain: A Pursuit

"Stanton, in a book that combines luminous travel writing with literary criticism, explores the territory of the writer's psyche and Spain, a country that he loved better than any other after his own."

—Joseph Coates, *Chicago Tribune*

"Edward Stanton's *Hemingway and Spain* is an informative, sensitive, beautiful book that is impossible to put down . . . It is an essential book . . . filled with knowledge and sensitivity and uncommon good sense . . ."

—James Nagel, *Modern Fiction Studies*

Wide as the Wind

"*Wide as the Wind* speaks to a fundamental truth: our need to protect the planet's environment."

—John Flenley and Paul Bahn,
authors of *The Enigmas of Easter Island*

"This novel transports us to an island world both outside time and urgently relevant to us in the 21st century."

—Leatha Kendrick, author of *Almanac of the Invisible*

VIDAS

For Bill,
without whom
this book
would not be.

¡Un gran abrazo!

[signature]

VIDAS

Deep in Mexico and Spain

Edward Stanton

Waterside Productions
Cardiff, California

Printed in the United States of America

First Printing, 2021

ISBN-13: 978-1-949003-47-5 print edition
ISBN-13: 978-1-949003-48-2 ebook edition

Waterside Productions
2055 Oxford Ave
Cardiff, CA 92007
www.waterside.com

A cuates y camaradas. Ellas, ellos saben.

Contents

No es el yo fundamental
eso que busca el poeta,
sino el tú esencial.

—Antonio Machado

... "You" ...
means I, one, you, as well as the you

Inside you constantly talk to.

—Frank Bidart

Before

The boy saw her running by the shore, so nimble that her feet hardly grazed the sand. Barefoot and bare-legged, she was older, maybe nine or ten. Behind her a red sun flared on the horizon. He watched the girl skip across the beach and turn into the wind, laughing, her blue-black hair swinging behind her as she splashed through the foam of a breaking wave.

Part One

New World

1. Concepción

When you saw him for the first time, Santa Ana winds were blowing heat and dust from the desert. He said with an ample gesture of his arm, as though his utterance referred to all the Californias, "*Hace calor.*" You had studied Spanish for a few months in school, but you did not understand those words that sounded so strange in the front yard of an American house in 1955. He explained them in a fatherly way, with patience and pride in his language, unlike anything you had ever heard or seen.

Concepción had been hired as gardener by the three sisters across the street. A volley of backfires from his 1947 Chevy pickup proclaimed his arrival once a week. As he parked by the curb, his engine coughed, sputtered and billowed smoke. His truck resembled an altar: a bloody crucifix on the dashboard, a rosary on the gearshift, a Virgin of Guadalupe in a place of honor on the rearview mirror. With great affection and irony he called it *El Poderoso*, The Powerful One.

He was short, ageless as an Indian, with a round face and a generous paunch. Concepción's uniform consisted of a white T-shirt and a sweat-stained bracero hat. You would not learn about his belief in dark powers until much later.

As the school bus returned to your neighborhood on Wednesday afternoons, you looked forward to seeing your new friend. Each time he taught you more words, phrases and idioms, which became gradually more ribald and complex. Talking with Concepción reminded you of conversations with your mother's Sicilian relatives. In fact some of his words seemed to echo their dialect, shaped in part by

Spaniards when they spread their language and empire across the Mediterranean.

Soon it was easier to understand him than your teacher at school, who spoke Spanish with a starched American accent. When you repeated one of Concepción's favorite expressions to her and the students, she bristled, arched her back and stood stiff as a saguaro cactus. She declared that it was wrong, and please see her after class. "Where in the devil did you learn *that?*" the teacher asked when the other students had gone. She inveighed against people who use vulgar language, charging you not to embarrass her again. Naturally this made you want to learn more and embarrass her again.

As your Spanish grew stronger, Concepción taught you part of his prodigious repertoire of Mexican folklore. It included a series of stories featuring a certain Don Cacahuate and Doña Cacahuata, Mr. and Mrs. Peanut, who were not legumes from just anywhere but from deep in Mexico, like your friend. *"Escucha nomás,"* Listen to this one, he started. Once upon a time the couple was competing with a gringo and a Chinaman to see who could last the longest in a room with a skunk. While the first two contestants took their turn, Mr. and Mrs. Peanut devoured delicious *tacos al pastor*, made from pork and three kinds of chiles, anchos, guajillos and pasillas. The American and the Chinese endured three minutes in the malodorous room. When Don Cacahuate and Doña Cacahuata entered, the poor skunk suffered a mere three seconds in their company before scampering away. Concepción threw back his head, his hat fell to the ground, he laughed hard and seized his belly with both hands.

He could describe the most ordinary facts in a style that only poets would affect in English. Someone who died a long time ago "has been eating earth for many years." A man on the verge of dying "has his soul in his mouth." Concepción often spoke about death, something you rarely discussed with your family or your friends. He saved the best for later.

He enjoyed calling our city by its complete, original name in Spanish, one of the most musical in the world: *El Pueblo de Nuestra*

Señora La Reina de Los Ángeles, Town of Our Lady Queen of the Angels. When those words fell from Concepción's tongue—he articulated carefully, savoring each vowel, consonant and syllable—the place where we lived at once acquired a vaster dimension, transfigured.

His glory was the proverb. He had one or more for every situation imaginable on earth, in heaven or hell. When Concepción uttered his adages, he would stop mowing, trimming or watering, rise to his full height of five feet-seven inches, remove his hat, gaze at you, the sky and the Santa Monica Mountains behind us, lift his right arm and speak in the rhythmic basso tones of an oracle the 500-year-old wisdom of the Spanish language filtered through the Mesoamerican mind. The proverbs tended to express the people's point of view, from the bottom up, the outside looking in, the small man reflecting on a corrupt world, commonsense sayings in the spirit of Sancho Panza. "Give the slow horse a head start," "Words don't bust your belly," "The devil is behind the cross."

Concepción had curious ideas on diverse subjects. Spanish he called the mother of languages; all others derive from it. He was convinced that twice as many women as men live on earth, and that this fortunate ratio is rising. Mexican ladies are the finest lovers, he confided, especially those with *"pata fina y ojos saltones,"* thin ankles and moon eyes—the most passionate, he added with a wink. Then Concepción told you about a brothel in Tijuana where a man announces at the door, *"Quiero romper,"* and they lead him to a room with a young girl whose virginity he would deflower. You had a little sister, and that story disturbed you so much that it must have showed on your face. Concepción noticed, perhaps realizing that he had gone too far: he smiled and put a big hand on your shoulder. He took a deep breath, sighing wistfully, *"Ay, el amor!"*

For some reason he had undertaken the duty of informing you about the facts of life, love and death. You could not grasp why he took the time to instruct a teenager who offered nothing in return except a willing ear. Concepción revealed that he had a daughter but not a son; were you the boy to whom he could offer his paternal guidance? Did he divine that he possessed a knowledge denied to young males in our time?

Concepción was never too occupied to pause and converse, to dwell on subjects trite or grave. He spoke of all things with equal reverence. Like a god he had endless leisure.

One August he missed a week at the three sisters' house. Their flowers wilted, weeds sprouted in their grass. The ladies were desperate. On a hot afternoon when the Santa Anas gusted again, Concepción returned. It was almost as if those dry winds from the east, the California siroccos, had blown him back into town.

Watching him take his rusty tools from the bed of *El Poderoso,* you asked, "Where have you been, Chon?" By this time the two of us were good friends, and you called him by his nickname.

"*Quihúbole* Eduardo." He hesitated. "A cousin of mine passed away in Tijuana."

"I'm sorry. Was he old?"

"No. He had just thirty-five *primaveras,* thirty-five springs."

"*Tan joven.* How did it happen?"

For once he did not seem anxious to talk. Concepción paused before speaking. "*Bueno.* It was a thing of the heart."

"A heart attack?"

"No. A woman had much spite toward him."

"I don't understand."

That's all it took for the raconteur and teacher in Concepción to tell his story. Besides he had said too much by now to stop. As usual he took off his bracero hat, mopped his brow, consulted the hills and clouds before launching his oration. "This woman was enamored of my cousin since years ago. She's ugly in spite of her mane of dark *cabello,*" he said, making a sinuous motion with one hand to suggest a woman's long, wavy hair. "Like a raven's wing, *negro azabache,* black and shiny as jet it was. When my cousin refused her love this woman began to twine the hairs from her head around his heart."

"How could she do that?"

"*Poco a poco,* a few locks at a time. She's a *bruja,* a sorceress who has many powers. So the hairs grew longer and thicker until my cousin felt pangs in his chest." He cupped his right hand, fingers like tree roots. "Finally the hairs grew so tight that they strangled his heart," he said. Concepción squeezed the fingers into a fist. "*La muerte, 'mano.* Death, brother."

The following Wednesday he admitted that he too was under the spell of a bruja in Tijuana. Concepción was feeling stabs of pain in the stomach, legs and spine, caused by the woman piercing a small effigy in the matching spots. He decided to consult a *curandera* or healer in Mexicali, a hundred miles or so farther east along the border, who gave him potions, pills and herbs to counteract the influence of the first woman. When you saw Concepción for the last time, the treatment continued.

He probably survived those spells of the man-killing witches of Baja California. Concepción was more defenseless against the women on this side of the border, where myth has no place. The sisters thought he worked too slowly and was absent too often. They asked him to leave.

You knew Concepción and his family would suffer: he was helpless like thousands of gardeners and braceros in the decade before César Chávez, Dolores Huerta and the United Farm Workers. Yet your friend took the news with serenity and the fatalism of his people.

"*Hay que cumplir,*" he said, looking at the clouds. "One must complete a job." Whether Concepción was addressing you, himself or the sky will never be known. "*Si Dios quiere,*" God willing, he said, "I'll find work at another house." For the last time he started mowing that lawn.

Watching him, you feared that we might not see each other again—you, a teenager too young to drive a car, the son of middle-class parents whose sphere was so distant from Concepción's in the barrio. All at once you realized how unlike we were, what strangers, brought together by the hazards of commerce and fortune.

He did not look up as he cut the grass. You felt powerless to aid your friend. How could the neighbors know how much Concepción needed that work, those thirty dollars a month? How could you explain to them the true stature and splendor of this man? How could you convince them that Concepción was more than a gardener, that he was a mentor, a companion, the keeper of an ancient vision, a human species endangered in a modern city? How could the three sisters understand they were stanching a wellspring of language, legend, humor, wisdom? For the first time you found yourself between two cultures, caught in the middle, divided between two ways of seeing the world.

He packed his tools in the bed of his truck. With tired brown eyes Concepción looked at you. He offered a rough, dirt-lined hand, saying, *"Hasta siempre, m'hijo,"* Until always, my son.

El Poderoso drove away, vanishing like the smoke from its tailpipes.

2. Lolo

L ed by a *coyote* or smuggler, he and his followers had managed to cross the border. Then they traveled in the bed of a truck or the trunk of a car to Los Angeles, where they boarded a boat for Santa Catalina, the island about twenty miles off the coast. There Lolo and his crew labored in the summers at a restaurant. They barely spoke English and returned faithfully to Mexico during the off-season. More than immigrants they were like swallows migrating to California from their winter roost in Jalisco. Few people cling to their country, language, food and customs like the Mexicans.

By luck you found a job as a busboy that summer at the restaurant, hoping to save enough to buy a car when you turned sixteen. There you met Lolo, captain of the dishwashing team, the oldest employee of The Pancake Cottage. He was forty-five with a mop of black hair and a build like a pyramid at Teotihuacán. He was proud of both his body and his curly head that glistened with pomade. Lolo (short for Heliodoro) was a man of parts: he had been an apprentice bullfighter, a mechanic, taxi-driver, barber. He was also the hardest-working man you had ever known. Each day between June and September he sweated for twelve hours in a steamy chamber beyond the kitchen, snatching meals there, renting a cheap room in a weathered bungalow with the members of his team. Living for almost nothing, he saved his money and returned each fall to his family and hometown, where he resumed his job as a barber. He shattered forever in your mind the cliché of the lazy Mexican.

During breaks at the restaurant you would walk to the muggy room to speak with Lolo. If there was a lull after breakfast, we would sit down to a quick meal at the end of the counter by the kitchen. The

Chicano cook from San Pedro, Art García, prepared *huevos rancheros* for the head dishwasher, swimming in chiles. In three summers at the Cottage Lolo had never eaten a single pancake or waffle. In this too he was like so many of his countrymen, loyal to their native cooking unto death.

As you wolfed down a stack of hotcakes, you asked him, "Why don't you try these?"

"I don't like that gringo stuff, Eduardo," Lolo said. "*Soy más mexicano que la tuna,*" I'm more Mexican than a prickly pear.

"We have *tunas* in California," you told him, "even on Santa Catalina. If you didn't work such long hours you'd have a chance to see them growing on the hills."

"Then I'm more Mexican than tequila," Lolo rejoined.

"Hell they bottle that stuff in the States now, man," Art chimed in, flashing his mustachioed smile that made him resemble a Chicano Clark Gable.

"Alright so I'm more Mexican than *pulque,*" Lolo countered, referring to the fermented sap of the maguey plant, never exported at the time. "Don't tell me they make that here," he added in triumph, laughing.

"Not yet," Art said.

With Lolo you practiced the tales and proverbs you had learned from Concepción. He could not believe that a fifteen year-old American kid knew stories about the peanut spouses, Don Cacahuate and Doña Cacahuata. Like your other friend Lolo took you under his wing, teaching you more words, turns of phrase, jokes. His favorite was a common greeting for a male friend in Mexico, when you ask, "*Cómo amaneciste?*"—in literal terms, How did you dawn this morning?, more loosely, How did you feel when you awoke? The answer to Lolo's question, his punch line, was "Like an old wagon cart, with its shaft in the air," delivered with a suitably priapic gesture.

He and his crew howled every time we exchanged the greeting, day after day, laughing each morning like the first. For them there was something outlandish about hearing these words from a gringo, hundreds, perhaps thousands of miles from rural Mexico where the joke must have arisen years ago. In the *machista* realm of the dishwashing room it was presumed that one always awoke with an erection.

Once in a while our days at The Pancake Cottage were harrowed by a raid. The cashier and waitresses alerted us when the suspicious characters appeared, normally a pair of crew-cut men in suits. As soon as they whispered "Immigration" to the busboys, we rushed to the dishwashing room, where we cried *"La Migra!"* to Lolo and his helpers. They tore off their wet rubber aprons, tossed them to us and fled through the back door into an alley. We started washing dishes as though we had been doing it all day. For the time being our waitresses would have to bus the tables.

After the agents had taken their time eating a hearty breakfast, then searching the kitchen and the dishwashers' room in vain, we walked to the alley and sounded the all-clear. Lolo's young teammates crawled out of the restaurant's fluted metal trash cans, their clothes smeared with eggs, sausages, pancakes and waffles, stained with butter, syrup and bacon grease. You volunteered to hunt for their captain, who had disappeared somewhere in Avalon, the island's only town. At his age Lolo refused to humiliate himself by hiding in a trash can.

You would find him sitting behind a palm tree by the bay, looking south toward the sea and Mexico. We walked back in silence.

Once we reached the alley, Lolo patted you on the shoulder without looking into your eyes. *"Gracias, 'mano."*

You remembered Concepción: he too had addressed you sometimes as *"'mano,"* short for "brother." At the end he had called you "son," and in truth he had been more of a father. Your new friend seemed like an uncle or an older brother. Both men were teachers. You had been unable to save Concepción's job, but now you were helping Lolo in a small way to keep his.

When he entered the restaurant through the back door, he was greeted like a hero returning from the wars. The other dishwashers, the cooks, waitresses and busboys gathered around Lolo.

"Chingada madre," Motherfucker, he would say. *"Hay que tener dignidad,"* A man must have a certain dignity.

Lolo, captain of his crew and our souls, taught us many lessons that summer. He showed us a man could have dignity and more, even if he was an illegal alien and a dishwasher.

3. Tijuana

Crossing the dry river bed, we saw the giant CARTA BLANCA billboard flashing against the night sky. It was Concepción's beer of choice, he had told you once; you remembered his stories about the witches of Tijuana. That sign announced the carte blanche, the open space, the savage freedom that you and other American males enjoyed beyond the border, where nothing was forbidden.

"We'll drink plenty of that brew," John said. Proud of his 1952 Oldsmobile and his new driver's permit, he steered us toward the center of town.

"T.J." you sighed.

"Don't say that," John urged. "You sound like the sailors and marines who come here." He had spent so much time in Tijuana that he considered it a second hometown.

"For me it's a term of affection."

Colors, sounds, smells all changed once we crossed the line: oranges, pinks, turquoises; shrill cries, motor scooters, cars, sizzle of frying food; odors of diesel, chiles, cilantro, candy, people, animals. The human warmth made it feel much hotter than San Diego, just fifteen miles to the north.

The Avenida de la Revolución teemed with tourists, pimps, hawkers and prostitutes. Vendors grilled tripe, pork, goat, chicken and beef on the curbs, filling the street with smoke and fumes. Young and old men lurched in and out of cabarets and hotels with hourly rates and names like París, La Cigüeña (The Stork) and Mona Lisa on their neon signs.

The red-light district seemed nearly bright enough to be noon. We cruised as far as the El Frontón Palacio, a white stucco building that looked more like a cathedral than a jai alai stadium. John parked on a side street sloping down from the busiest thoroughfare in Upper or Lower California.

A new world unfolded for us on the Avenida. There the real revolution was not the one marked on street signs, which had occurred in Mexico about fifty years earlier, but the turbulence of teenage boys swept into the whirlpool of desire. Unlike American cities where erotic life was almost invisible, Tijuana showed it openly, as it had been displayed in other places for millennia. It was our Babylon, Gomorrah, Calcutta, our poor Rome and Paris. It made no difference whether you bought or sold: everyone was assumed to take part in the exchange, everything had its price. The city's life revolved around the sexual trade.

Tijuana offered us liberation from our ravenous lust and a knowledge we could not acquire in the United States of the 1950s. Although our two countries were very different, in a way we resembled our brothers in Mexico, where the cult of virginity among nubile girls forced young men to seek initiation in bordellos. It had been that way for centuries in parts of the world.

How many times did we walk up and down the sidewalks of the Avenida de la Revolución, that night and others, under the neon lights, the garish signs flashing on and off? How many bars did we enter, those dark caves prohibited to us at home, how many Carta Blancas, Dos Equis, Bohemias, Moctezumas, Tecates, Cuba libres, gin and tonics, whisky and sodas did we drink in the half-light? How many winking barkers with their pencil-line mustaches, fedoras, gaudy coats and sunglasses accosted us, "The next chow begeen rite now," "Coam see most sexy girls all Mehico first tine Tijuana," "You like dirty peetchers, dirty moovie?" "You wan foak nice yown girl?" How many cabarets, night clubs, striptease joints, dives, *casas de putas*: the Blue Fox where clients sucked the bitterness from the dancers' sex onstage, the unnamed brothel where clients announced "Quiero romper" as Concepción had told you, the only thing broken—our hearts at the sight of those tender-aged girls, meek,

30

wide-eyed offerings at the altar of male desire? How many gloomy passages did we follow, how many red or green walls did we pass, how many rooms furnished with a cot, a plastic bidet and washstand, a single, fluttering light bulb suspended from the ceiling? How many old women sitting in strategic corners, priestesses of love who dispensed matches, cigarettes, towels, ointments and condoms, dreaming of their own youthful nights never to be repeated? How many girls from the provinces, some of them still wobbly in high heels, telling us they sent money each month to their families, who believed or pretended to believe their daughters were holding down honest jobs in Baja California? How many older prostitutes who could barely squeeze into their tight, spangled dresses, their flat butts and round tummies ready to explode from their girdles, sitting on barstools and drinking watered-down cocktails in tall glasses, the shadows forgiving for a few more weeks, months or a year the harsh grooves that flared from their nostrils to the edges of their mouth? How many starts and stops, how many illusions, failures, raptures, surprises?

After several visits to Tijuana you met Alfa, a young woman from the Gulf of Tehuantepec. Happy to find a customer who spoke Spanish, she led you to a little room in the rear of the bordello where she lived with her baby boy, Nazario. Most of the chamber was taken up by a small bed, a vibrantly-painted wooden cradle and a makeshift altar with colored prints of a gory Christ, a Virgin of Guadalupe and a black Virgin of Montserrat, patroness of women in childbirth, Alfa said. The sole missing god seemed to be Eros. The room hardly had an atmosphere for making love.

Before long you discovered that Alfa wanted to find relief from the hordes of marines, sailors, students and tourists who stormed in every weekend from Camp Pendleton and San Diego. While we drank tea brewed in tamarind flowers one evening, she told her story. She had been brought up in a large family dominated by her father, who punished the children by making them kneel in the sun and hold rocks over their head until they collapsed in exhaustion, or by giving them *cuerazos,* lashes with a waxed strip of leather used for hitching bulls to an oxcart. When Alfa turned fifteen, soon after her *quinceañera* party, she learned that her father had arranged a marriage between her and one of his cronies, a man more than fifty years old. In the meantime she was secretly visiting a boy her own age who worked on a construction crew in the nearest town, Santa María del Mar. Once she got pregnant by him, Alfa did not wish to marry either man, because in both cases she would have had to undergo the humiliating test for purity: a white handkerchief inserted into her vagina after the wedding night, then displayed in public. "Anyhow," she said, "they were both *pinches cabrones*," fucking bastards.

Her mother gave Alfa enough cash to buy a bus ticket to Mexico City and Tijuana, more than two thousand miles away, as far as she could travel without leaving the country. She found work easily at a brothel on the Avenida de la Revolución: her brown complexion, her black eyes and Zapotec features made her stand out among the other girls, mostly mestizas from central or northern Mexico. Hawkers touted her with a rhyming jingle, *"la tehuana de Tijuana,"* the Tehuantepec girl of Tijuana. In the months before her belly became too prominent, she earned enough to pay for a doctor, then a *partera*, a midwife. The other girls at the house chipped in to cover the rent until Alfa could resume her job. When she started work several weeks after the birth, her companions took turns caring for the baby.

Now Nazario was almost one year-old. Every three or four hours his mother would return to feed him in that room, a nursery and shrine. While Alfa suckled her baby wrapped in Zapotec blankets, you sat next to her on a bumpy cot, captivated. Nazario fell asleep with one of his mother's dark nipples in a corner of his mouth, leaving her achingly swollen with milk. Then she offered you a taut, smooth brown breast. *"Toma, alíviame, Lalo,"* she would say, using the nickname for Eduardo. You sucked the sweet, bluish-white milk from her warm nipple.

That was an unforgotten night you enjoyed in the summer of 1959 with the young mother from Tehuantepec. From Alba you learned that language can be a key, that it can unlock doors closed to most foreigners, perhaps even to other native speakers. "*Los mexicanos*—they live here and can hurt us more than the gringos," she said. In a couple of years, you guessed, she would also have lines of bitterness around her mouth.

After nights and dawns of outrageous drinking and insatiable yearnings, you and John would sleep through the morning in the car or in one of the cheap hotels off Revolución, part flophouses, part whorehouses. When we woke it was time for a late lunch: *menudo*, tripe soup spiced with hot peppers, the world's best dish for a hangover; *enchiladas verdes*; fillets of *huachinango*, red snapper; abalone steaks washed down with Tecate and lemon juice.

After our first Sunday meal in Tijuana, John ordered two black coffees spiced with cinnamon. As we drank it, he asked, "You're coming to the *corrida*, Ed?"

"I guess so."

"You don't want to see the bulls killed, right? Like so many Americans."

"You know how much I love animals. My family's had dogs as long as I can remember."

"You have to get that idea out of your head, man. A fighting bull's not a pet—it's as different from cattle on a ranch as a wolf's different from a dog." You swilled from the bottom of your cup, tasting the coffee grains on your tongue. "It's also the only animal in the world that kills out of instinct, not hunger."

"Yeah I know all the arguments for and against the corrida, John. Maybe some day I'll have *afición* like you."

"Not many Americans have as much passion for the bulls as I do," he laughed, but turned quickly serious. "Here we are gorging ourselves while the *toreros* are fasting."

"Why?"

"So their intestines will be empty in case they're gored and need surgery." Hearing those words, with a full stomach and a heady buzz from the beer, your qualms about the corrida seemed petty.

Then it was time for the bullfight at four o'clock sharp in the afternoon. Heading up Revolución with the images of the night still seething in our heads, we bought cigars at a sidewalk stand, lit them and moved with the crowds to the old El Toreo de Tijuana, the downtown bullring.

As we watched those corridas, your friend taught you most of what you know about the bulls and the men who meet them. Together we saw the death of animals from Mexican *ganaderías,* ranches whose bloodlines descended from Spain, with sonorous names like Piedras Negras, Mimihuapan, Pastejé, La Punta, San Mateo, Tequisquiapan, La Laguna, Torrecilla, Atenco, Coaxamalucan. That season and others we saw the Mexican *matadores* Fermín Rivera, mercurial Luis Procuna, Manuel Capetillo, Alfredo Leal, Humberto Moro, intrepid Joselito Huerta; the Venezuelans César Farraco and the Girón brothers, the Spaniards Antonio Bienvenida and Antonio Ordóñez, who was wounded by a bull one afternoon a few seconds after it charged from the gate into the dazzling, barbarous sun of Mexico. In the Toreo de Tijuana you began to understand, slowly, the afición felt by John and others around us.

Fighting bull.

34

In the car afterwards, our bodies warmly tired, our faces lined with dust, we inched forward in the long line of vehicles to the border. We felt either the purged emptiness that follows a good corrida or the sense of betrayal after a poor one. Passing warehouses, factories, stores and streets without end, we snaked up the coast highway toward Los Angeles. We were too fatigued, we had too many memories in our head to chat. Both you and John knew we had lived and learned more in a weekend than in months at home. Those days and nights in Tijuana, that wasteland, beloved and despised outpost, were changing us fast.

We probably didn't know that by driving over the line between Upper and Lower, Alta and Baja California, we were crossing a frontier in our minds and bodies more crucial than the boundary between nations. Nor did we think the formal ceremony of blood spilled on the sand, amid the most astonishing violence, tedium or beauty, was somehow related to that other rite of man and woman, its anguish, repulsion or ecstasy. How could we know, two sixteen year-old kids, that we were already living the greatest mysteries, love and death?

4. Laura

You wanted to get farther away from home, farther than Tijuana with its absurd grotesque of the U.S. and Mexico, beyond the border and Baja California, deeper into the country. The city of Saltillo lay on a slope of the Sierra Madre Oriental, just north of the central plateau, about 5,000 feet high. There you found a boarding-house with a courtyard on Calle Xicoténcatl of sacred memory.

Your room opened onto the light-filled patio with a gurgling well, shade trees, cracked flower pots, a colossal *zaguán* or foyer with an immense, carved wooden portal. The courtyard was the hub of life for everyone in the house: the landlords Don Alfonso and Doña Hortensia; their daughter, her husband and their children; Panchita, a plump Indian woman who did most of the shopping, cooking and cleaning; a bachelor who taught Latin and Greek at several schools to make ends meet; uncountable dogs, cats and birds in cages. And then there was the woman who scandalized our whole house and neighborhood. Laura.

She must have been in her fifties, but she moved with the grace of a young woman. She wrapped her lean frame in shabby scarves and shawls and wore long, rustling, flowered skirts that glided over the cobblestones of the patio. Although her hair was disheveled in front, Laura gathered it into a neat Psyche knot at the nape of her slender model's neck. Every evening she left the house and did not return until late in the night, at dawn, in the morning or the next afternoon. Laura's arrivals and departures were staged in the grand style to attract attention and awaken anyone with the nerve to be asleep on such portentous occasions.

A few days after settling into the boardinghouse, you enrolled in a Spanish-language school for the summer. Walking to class one morning, you passed a cantina on the corner and spotted Laura through the louvered, swinging doors. She was seated at a table, alone.

She recognized you, calling in a voice that seemed too husky for her ethereal body: "*Vecino!* Neighbor! *Ven a acompañarme,*" Come keep me company.

You walked inside, past the bartender who was sweeping the floor with sawdust. There were no customers except Laura.

Two bootblacks crouched on the steel footrail below the bar, their little shoeshine boxes at their sides. They asked, jumping to their feet, "*Le boleo?*" Want a shine? in the forlorn mumble used by those boys who repeat the same question hundreds of times a day. There must be more bootblacks in Mexico than anywhere in the world. It may be the only country with a special verb for polishing shoes.

When you reached Laura's table, she asked, "Eduardo, will you invite a lady to a drink?" Her breath immersed you in the night's effluvium. On her table stood an empty shot glass.

"Of course, *vecina.*"

"Sergio! Bring us a pair," she told a second barman who was removing bottles of Bohemia from a wooden case. Seeing her close, you noticed the glisten of tears in Laura's eyes.

Sunlight slanted through the doors and windows, striking the time-stained mirror and rows of bottles behind the bar: Souza, José Cuervo, Tequila Añejo, Mezcal Xicoténcatl, named like your street for the indigenous warrior; Anís del Mono with a devil on its label; Johnny Walker Red, local wines and brandies from Parras de la Fuente.

The man brought us a round of tequila with two saucers, one filled with salt and the other with halves of lime. "*Salud,* vecino," Laura said, raising her glass in a toast and quaffing her drink as though it were water. "By the way do you mind if I call you by our nickname for Eduardo?"

"No."

"Guess what it is."

"Lalo," you replied, thinking of Alfa.

"You're learning, vecino."

Your shot did not go down as smoothly as hers that morning, but it would not be our last drink together. She taught you to chase tequila with dabs of salt and juice from the lime, sucked after each swig, making the alcohol taste almost sweet. Other times we would alternate with *sangrita* (no, not *sangría*), a reviving blend of fruit juices spiced with chiles.

"Sangrita works nearly as well as menudo for hangovers," Laura counseled.

You arrived late to class that day and others. Just as Concepción and Lolo had enlightened you more than teachers in school, Laura would educate you more than *maestros* in the language program. She took you under her wings of tarnished feathers.

While the jukebox played songs on those luminous mornings in the corner cantina, Laura would turn nostalgic and tell stories of her youth. Listening to *rancheras* and *boleros,* getting drunk, wallowing in the pain of unhappy love is a collective pastime in Mexico. Hundreds of songs sing of going on sprees, emptying bottle after bottle, drinking oneself into oblivion, all for love, usually lost:

Cómo son lindas estas borracheras . . .

How nice are these binges . . .

You did not have old loves to remember, but you grasped the music's appeal, as enticing as a warm, soft bunk when you're supposed to be in class or at work. One could cultivate that sentiment for a lifetime. Whole nations do.

Each time Laura evoked the past, her eyes sparkled and revealed the young girl behind her wrinkled mask. In her prime she must have been a startling beauty. Even with her body wasted by long nights, by drink and years, she preserved an air of faded elegance.

Like most femmes fatales she had known many men in her life but only one great love. The facts of that affair remained unclear. Laura stammered when she had drunk too much, and your ears were still learning the rhythms of speech in northern Mexico. You had the impression that the man may have committed suicide. Yet Laura could have fused his story with another about Manuel Acuña, the poet from Saltillo who's supposed to have killed himself after writing a poem to his beloved. She would often recite his famed "Nocturno a Rosario":

> *¡Pues bien! Yo necesito*
> *decirte que te adoro,*
> *decirte que te quiero*
> *con todo el corazón . . .*

> Well then! I need to say
> that I adore you,
> that I love you
> with my whole heart . . .

Laura knew this poem and dozens more by heart. If the juke-box ran out of songs, she would stand unsteadily and recite, fondling the air with her blue-veined, bony hands. She declaimed works by Gustavo Adolfo Bécquer, by Sor Juana Inés de la Cruz, Amado Nervo and all the nation's classics. She sang corridos, ballads, especially those about La Llorona, the legendary woman of Mexican folklore who haunts lonely spots at night, weeping for lost loves: *"Ay de mi Llorona, Llorona."*

As Laura chanted, a few lingering customers, the bootblacks of the moment and the bleary-eyed bartenders would turn silent.

Passers-by stopped to peek inside the cantina and listen: newsvendors with morning papers bundled in their arms, delivery boys carrying crates of Coca Cola, Fanta and Tri Naranjus; servants on their way to market, crippled beggars dragging their poor bodies along with crutches. In the summer of 1960 the oral tradition was alive in Saltillo, Coahuila, México.

If the onlookers requested an encore, Laura would sing her favorite ranchera:

> *No vale nada la vida,*
> *la vida no vale nada.*
> *Comienza siempre llorando*
> *y así llorando se acaba.*
>
> Life is worth nothing,
> It's not worth a thing.
> It begins with crying
> and also ends in tears.

As long as she kept the verses flowing with rhyme and meter, the tragedienne could hold her public in thrall. But if she forgot the words of a poem or the lyrics of a song, Laura would collapse in her chair, cover her head and cry her eyes out. *"Ay, Lalo, soy una mujer fracasada,"* I'm a failed woman, she sobbed through her tears.

Between performances Laura talked about her past. "Modesty apart," she confessed, "I was irresistible as a young girl, vecino."

"Ya lo creo," I can believe it.

"Thank you, Lalo. You treat me like a *caballero*—a real gentleman you are. Anyway in school I suffered abuse from priests and nuns." She winced either from the memory or the shot of tequila that she had just swallowed.

"Detrás de la cruz está el diablo," The devil's behind the cross, you said, recalling one of Concepción's adages.

"*Ándale*, Lalo. After the Revolution the *curas*, the priests, the monks and nuns weren't allowed to wear vestments or habits on the street. Served the cabrones right! I haven't crossed the threshold of a church since I graduated from school."

Laura was the first anticlerical woman you would meet in Mexico. She was also a raconteur who rivaled Concepción. Quoting the Spanish proverb, she would say, "Good conversation is food for the soul."

She could find a story in every person who entered our cantina. When a ghostly beggar, an Indian wrapped in a *rebozo*, passed through one morning, Laura said, "*Fíjate bien*, vecino. That man works on a ranch yet he has to beg in order to feed his family. Notice his eyes." When the Indian passed our table, he glanced at us with palms extended. His glacial look made you shiver. "That's the kind of citizen our Church and our caciques have created," Laura said. "One night he'll stab somebody or wake up with a knife in his heart".

Another day Panchita, the servant at our house, passed the cantina on her way to market. The portly woman peeked inside, spotted you at Laura's table and scurried away. By evening the landlords had learned the dreadful news.

Feeling that she had a parental responsibility for her teenaged American boarder, Doña Hortensia summoned you to the living room. It was your first and only entry into that forbidden sanctuary whose shutters remained closed day and night, where incense smoldered, where votive candles burned beneath an image of the Virgin of Guadalupe.

The landlady sighed. "I suppose she asks for money, Eduardo?" She did not need to mention Laura's name.

"Once in a while." A candle sputtered and a bird's song came from the patio. Suddenly you wanted to be outside.

"I'm going to give you a piece of motherly advice, hijo. For your own good and hers, stay away from her. *Es una mujer perdida*," She's a lost woman, Doña Hortensia lamented. "Every month she's behind on her rent, she promises to pay but usually finds an excuse. You

42

should not lend her one *centavo*. Actually you should not see her at all." Rising on her toes, the woman cupped her hands and whispered in your ear: "I've been trying to get rid of her for a long time—so I can rent her room to another *gabacho*—I mean North American. Your compatriots always pay on time."

You did not heed her counsel any more than you had obeyed the teacher's warning about Concepción. Doña Hortensia cared more about the repute and solvency of her boardinghouse than your probity or pocketbook. You felt the fatal allure of ripe, forbidden fruit, sensing that Laura had more to impart, more vitality than all the other residents and their animals together.

The incident confirmed what you were learning about Mexico: it's a machista society in public, a matriarchy at home. Doña Hortensia, with Panchita as her loyal informer, ruled the roost at number 111, Calle Xicoténcatl Sur. Sometimes her husband Don Alfonso, the nominal patriarch, pretended to hold sway, twisting his white, Porfirio Díaz-mustache as he mouthed empty orders around the house. Nobody bothered to listen. Everyone knew the women were in charge.

They were also the guardians of religion, the ones who attended Mass, who kept the faith by lighting candles beneath the Virgin in the living room, the house's inner sanctum. If Doña Hortensia and Panchita governed the home, the *Guadalupana*—Mother of Mexico, Patroness of the Americas—ruled the nation, the hemisphere and the world for those people. You did not think about these things as much as breathe them with the incense, see them in the light of the votive candles.

The boardinghouse was a miniature reflection of the whole country, where God the Father and Christ stand as titular heads of the Church, while the people's worship centers on the Virgin Mary, *María Santísima*, Most Holy Mary, *Nuestra Señora*, Our Lady. She and motherhood are so hallowed that a careless use of the word *madre* in Mexico can be more dangerous than a curse. Speakers soften the incendiary term by using the more familiar *mamá* or the diminutive *mamacita.* On the other hand their everyday conversation bristles with references to *La Chingada,* "the Fucked One," the Nahua woman who betrayed her people to the Spaniards. Doña Marina, as she was known to the invaders, assisted them in defeating the Aztecs, who called her La Malinche. She slept with the conqueror Cortés and gave birth to one of the first mestizos, offspring of mixed blood. Her crime was cleansed in part by a second mother, the Guadalupana, who manifested herself to a poor peasant near Mexico City as the angel Gabriel had appeared to a humble girl in Judea about 1,500 years before. But in some ways Mexicans are still a people of orphans whose wounds have never healed, who need a personal and communal mother in the form of María Santísima.

Doña Hortensia's hypocrisy and Laura's history did not keep you from visiting churches in Saltillo and other towns. The Baroque, Rococo and Churrigueresque façades enclosed somber, cool interiors, so bracing after the glaring heat outdoors. Aromas of incense penetrated your nose and infused your lungs. A few older men, but mostly women recited the Ave Maria over and over. As your eyes adapted to the semi-darkness, you observed how many were dressed in mourning, head to foot.

Above the rows of candles shimmering in the gloom, behind the altars encrusted with bossed leaves and tendrils, you gazed at sumptuous pilasters, cornices, vaults and domes; reredos like fantastic grottos of wood, stucco, porphyry, gold and silver; a cornucopia of vines, flowers, fruits, trees, birds, animals, serpents, fish; centaurs, gargoyles, chimeras, griffins, unknown creatures; golden reliefs, moldings, marquetry, scrolls, curlicues, intaglios, escutcheons. Walking down the nave toward the main altar, you passed a forest of columns, chapels with portraits or statues of saints in marble or polychrome wood, fat-buttocked Cupids, wide-winged cherubim and seraphim with faces of the sun and moon, Christs with gashes blossoming on their ankles and wrists, Virgins of Guadalupe in various local incarnations, their hands clasped in prayer, their head bowed to one side beneath their blue mantel of stars, their gown embroidered with roses, their feet cradled in a crescent moon supported by an angel. O sanctuaries of Mexico, women in black, odors of frankincense, candles flickering in the shadows, bleeding Christs and tender Guadalupanas.

Raised in America's male-oriented Protestant churches, you were drawn to the nurturing, female religion of Mexico. Somehow being in these temples was a way of returning to your ancestors, to the beliefs of your Spanish great-great-grandmother and your mother's Sicilian forebears, relinquished once she married your father, who was a reformed German through and through. Compared to the severe, barren, overlit chapels of your childhood, those penumbral shrines embraced you in the warmth of a maternal faith and a tribal worship.

Walking into the ruthless sunlight, you saw the ragged children, the armies of dwarves and cripples. Some sat on the stone steps with their brown palms cupped as though for communion. Like most foreigners you were repelled by the brazen opulence of the Church amid the general misery of the people. But you were learning that in Mexico devotion and suffering are wedded. In some ways the beggars on the steps were just as hallowed as the clergy indoors. You gave alms to those poor souls in exchange for one of the world's loveliest benedictions: "*Vaya usted con Dios.*"

As the semester approached its end, you invited Laura for a farewell drink one night.

After the first round she asked, "Lalo, shall we have *la penúltima?*"

"What's that?"

"We never say 'the last drink'—for us it's always 'the next-to-last.'"

"Ándele."

Laura surprised you by paying for several rounds of tequilas. Then she asked, "Would you accompany a *dama*, a lady to her home?"

"Isn't it early for you, vecina?"

"I have not been escorted home by a gentleman for a long time. I would be grateful."

Rising from the chair, you gave an arm to Laura; hers seemed light as a bird's wing. When we reached our house at Calle Xicoténcatl, Don Alfonso opened the tall, creaking portal. *"Muy buenas noches,"* he whispered with a conspiratorial smile and a gesture that must have meant, Hurry up and go inside before *she* spots you.

But Doña Hortensia was ever vigilant. As we crossed the patio, our landlady emerged by the well, standing with her legs planted on the flagstone and her arms akimbo, like some stalwart peasant woman in a painting by Diego Rivera.

Her eyes burned holes in your back while you held Laura in a final embrace. "Hasta siempre," your friend said with tears in her eyes. Memories of that phrase gushed through your head like the water surging from the well at our side.

After returning to Los Angeles, you wrote Laura several times. Those letters went unanswered. Months later Doña Hortensia wrote to say that her boarder had disappeared, "without paying her rent, of course."

Where were you Laura, vecina, *compañera*? Where had you gone, my Llorona? In what bar, in what sunny cantina were you drinking tequila with salt and limes, reciting poems, singing ballads and remembering loves lost forever?

5. Zanahorio

He called you *Colacho,* Milk-Brother, slang for children nursed by the same woman. In fact we would be like brothers who had sucked from a single breast. We would walk, ride buses and hitchhike from one end of Mexico to another, sleep in beds of the same trucks, beds of the same flophouses rooms and without beds on beaches from Ensenada to Veracruz and the Yucatán.

His name was Gustavo but they called him *Zanahorio,* Carrot or Carrot-Top. In Hispanic folklore redheads are supposed to be born mischievous. The folk hit the mark in Zanahorio. No people use nicknames more widely and more ingeniously than the Mexican.

Initiation rites in brothels sometimes created a passing bond between a man and woman, nearly always between him and his companions. You had felt a close tie to John, tempered by American reserve, on our journeys to Tijuana. You would feel it fully with Zanahorio in a country that fostered a deeper friendship between young men. We had met by chance one day in Saltillo, where we spent time together that summer. When classes ended, Gustavo invited you to travel around the country, promising to show you a different Mexico. *"No has visto nada, Colacho,"* he said, You haven't seen anything.

His ancestors came from venerable Castilian lines, Dávilas and Ortegas. He did not have a drop of indigenous blood. Gustavo's carrot-head towered over you and his other friends. With his height, his shock of red hair and light complexion, he could pass for an American as long as he did not open his mouth to speak. He boasted that he hardly knew a word of English.

Gustavo's older sister had married into a prestigious dynasty, descendants of Francisco Madero, architect of the Mexican Revolution and president of the country. Her husband was a senator who spent most of his time in the capital, while she stayed in the family's Saltillo home. Like so many in Mexico it was run by women—mother, sister and maids. Your friend's father, who apparently lived in town with a mistress, never surfaced there. To mention his name would have violated an unspoken taboo. Since Gustavo was the only son, the one male in the house, his mother and older sister pampered him. He had been expelled from every high school in Saltillo, private and public, yet in their eyes he was still Gustavito, little Gustavo who could do no evil. For the maids he was *el señorito*, the young master of the house, whose wishes were their commands. For everyone else he was Zanahorio.

He walked with the swagger of a boy whose family could always bail him out of trouble, who knew that he was attractive to women and wore the most striking pair of boots in Mexico. They were made of softest black leather, hand-sewn, notched and pinked with tracery, covered with a silver filigree where his initials were engraved in Baroque script: G.D.O. As if the boots did not already arouse enough attention, Gustavo had nailed steel tips to the soles, making them click and proclaim themselves from thirty yards as he paced down a street or sidewalk.

One day you asked him to borrow the magic boots. They fit more or less well but without Zanahorio's unmistakable saunter—the way he would swing out his leading foot from his ankle then tap the ground with the toe of the trailing boot. They sounded dead on the pavement. It was the last time you would ask to wear them.

Those boots and your tennis shoes walked the roads of Mexico from the Río Bravo to the Guatemalan border. If it was too far to walk, we hitched rides in cars, jeeps, pickups, cattle trucks and trailer trucks, or we rode gaudy-colored buses with grandiose names like "La Estrella del Norte" and "La Flecha del Sur," their dashboards and windshields adorned with Virgins, saints and crucifixes, their seats

48

occupied by women, men, children and beasts, while young boys hung out the doors, their shirt sleeves and trousers flapping in the breeze.

We traveled from the Texas border south between the ranges of the Sierra Madre into the high, fertile valley of Anáhuac, passing under the shadow of snow-topped volcanoes, Ixtaccíhuatl and Popocatépetl, with sloping fields on their flanks, forests farther up, their peaks shrouded in smoke, fog or thunderheads. Then we cut west to the beaches of the Pacific, Zihuatanejo and Mazatlán, or sometimes east to the Gulf of Mexico, crossing through Puebla, Oaxaca and Chiapas, the jungles of Mayan country in Tabasco, Campeche, the Yucatán, finally returning to where we had started by different routes, voracious for new landscapes, villages, towns, cities, peoples.

We traveled on asphalt roads, cement roads, gravel roads, dirt roads, roads pitted by potholes and craters, flooded roads, always roads with dead animals, dogs, chickens, cats, donkeys, horses, armadillos, iguanas and snakes while the *zopilotes,* the buzzards and vultures floated dreamily above, waiting. We saw the roadside shrines and crosses marking spots where people had died, decorated with more Virgins, Christs and flowers—live, paper or plastic flowers that made of death a display and a warning. You were beginning to understand the Mexican cult of mortality that you had merely glimpsed through Concepción's stories and proverbs.

We passed peasants nodding on the backs of horses or burros, men and women wrapped in rebozos against the mountain cold, girls and boys in huaraches, holding up live or dead armadillos for sale; towns in fiesta with bright flags, banners and paper streamers, bands playing patriotic songs and *pasodobles,* dignitaries decked out in suits and sashes, drunks dancing or reeling down the alleys, ferris wheels turning against the big-clouded sky, hawkers selling taquitos, beer, sodas and sweets under trees in the plazas, open-air markets piled with vegetables, fruits, meats, blankets, *serapes,* earthenware the same hue as the natives who sold them, who squatted on the ground, immobile as statues, their bare or sandaled feet coated with dried mud. We were in the heart of Mexico evoked by one of its writers: "its villages, its churches, the world of dust and cheap brandy and dirty tricks played on the disgraced Indian by the crafty mestizo, owner of store, brothel and pawnshop."

Although we never confessed it to one another, women were the goal and purpose of our wanderings. When we reached a new town in late afternoon, covered with grime from the road, we found a place to sleep, washed, changed clothes then headed straight into the *zócalo* or *alameda*, the main square with a bandstand in the middle, to join the *paseo*, the evening stroll or promenade. Women and girls, young and old paraded in a circle, often in pairs, holding arms or hands, while men and boys walked in the other direction, perhaps arm in arm too, everyone talking to their companions or pretending to talk while observing the oncoming pedestrians, sometimes greeting them, the boys saying *piropos,* amorous compliments to the girls, hoping for the prize of a blush, a glance, a smile or at most a few words. Since young people could seldom be together in private, most of their passion was reserved for this. It charged the air like the thunderstorms that rumbled unfailingly through central Mexico on summer afternoons. The raising of an eyelid by a centimeter, a toss of hair, the curl of a lip, a flash of teeth could provoke utter, momentary joy.

We felt like remarkable newcomers in each town, where we were soon known as *los güeros,* the fair-skinned ones. The local girls wanted to meet the tall, red-headed boy from Saltillo with the funny nickname and the magnetic boots, who traveled with a Spanish-speaking friend from El Norte. But their mothers, grandmothers, aunts and older sisters—the Mexican matriarchy—mobilized instantaneously to protect those vestal virgins, mistrustful of males in general, outsiders in particular and foreigners *ni hablar*: they watched us with a thousand eyes. Since those women knew nothing about Gustavo's family or yours, about our friends, homes or social class, they could not determine if we belonged to the privileged group of eligible young men. In short they could not establish if we were *muchachos serios,* "serious" suitors for their daughters, granddaughters, nieces or sisters. This drove them crazy, so they excluded us from the fortunate elite. For our part, forever on the move from one town to another, we did not have patience or leisure for the prescribed ceremony of courtship, a plodding, protracted ritual from which we might have emerged days or weeks later with the paltry reward of a pressed hand or—O rapture!—a furtive kiss. No, by any standard we were not serious candidates for those chaste *señoritas.*

We tried calling on some of them in their homes, but we rarely penetrated those bastions: high walls spiked with shards of glass, prodigious, brass-knobbed portals, windows and balconies barred with wrought iron. Not to mention the wary guards, servants and duennas who watched over those maidens. As the writer Paul Theroux says, Mexican life is "a vision of battlements."

After the paseo we had dinner, washed down with several beers for courage. Then we took to the streets, asking for the *zona* or *zumbido*—the "zone" or "buzz"—the quarter where anything you could imagine or afford was allowed. In those badlands, usually located in the outskirts where paved streets turned to gravel, dirt or mud, lit by a couple of streetlamps, or unlit, we found bars, nightclubs, striptease joints, bordellos where life began late at night and continued until early morning, the always-fresh, beautiful Mexican *madrugada*. In those places you could watch stage shows where women masturbated with a banana, a chorizo or a live duck, made Coke bottles or a pair of eyeglasses vanish in their organs, copulated with a dwarf, offered their sex to customers on a stage, warning them under their breath, "*No muerdas,* Don't bite, *corazón.*" We were just a mile or two from downtown and the paseo, light-years in every other way.

In some towns like Piedras Negras, across the border from Eagle Pass, you could walk along the sidewalk of wooden planks, suspended over the dust and mire, and see women lying on their beds through open windows, close enough to reach in and touch their half-dressed bodies. You could strike a deal right there, climb through the window or go around the back if you were not in a rush. You could buy any drug on the street, in the bars or *taquerías*, from marijuana to peyote and aphrodisiacs. When money exchanged hands, it was almost invariably between men, mestizos—brokers, pimps, go-be-tweens—who controlled those barrios, so different from the matri-archal homes of Mexico.

Driven by the lord of desire, you followed Gustavo into that noc-turnal, alien world, so much more savage than Tijuana. Together we entered the zonas and zumbidos of Ciudad Juárez, Nuevo Laredo, Matamoros and Piedras Negras on the Texas line, then south to our home base of Saltillo, to Monterrey and Torreón, through the heartland in San Luis Potosí, Aguascalientes and Querétaro, the high plateau and Mexico City, east to Puebla, Orizaba and Veracruz, farther south to Oaxaca and Tehuantepec (you remembered Alfa), east again to Chiapas, Tabasco, Campeche and the Yucatán. How you remember those towns and others, the women, their enfolding presence: the patient ones whose gentle hands led you into love, the hurried ones who had already become images of your past. How you cherish the memory of Olga in Fresnillo, Magdalena of Pachuca, Elvira of Irapuato, Dolores of Toluca, Luz in Tlaxcala! How often you recall them, your craving turned to pity for those girls trapped in the gears of a patriarchal machine. But if you are seventeen, at large in Mexico, seeing new things and learning every hour, any cheap dive, any impulse or encounter is pure as the snows of Popocatépetl, stained by hot ashes.

Toward the end of summer we took a precarious route to the Gulf along the Cumbres de Maltrata, where a vehicle plunged off the cliffs every week or so. It was part of the country's violent topography that lies in wait for disaster, evoked by one of its best writers: "bot-tomless canyons . . . treacherous peaks, winds clashing amid deliri-ous contours; sudden deserts and a thousand pyramids disguised as harmless hills."

In Orizaba we came close to our end. It was late on a steaming September night, nearly dawn. Most places in the zone had locked their doors and lowered their aluminum grills or shutters. At last we found a bar where a *jarocho* band was playing their treble-pitched harp and guitars. By the time we sat down to order beers, even stragglers were going home. Wooden fans on the ceiling, tired as the music and the night, flailed the torpid air.

A raucous group of young men were the only other patrons. From the far side of the room they stared at us from a large table, laughing, pointing our way. Some of their words reached us through the discordant, smoky air: *"Pinches gabachos . . . cabrones . . . hijos de la rechingada . . ."* Damn gringos . . . bastards . . . sons of the fucking whore.

"We're closing so you'll have to pay now," the waitress warned as she served us Superior in pint glasses. "Watch out for those *ricachos,* those rich boys at the other table."

You had never seen Zanahorio look so disturbed. "How are we going to get out of this one, Colacho?" he asked without expecting a reply. "It's five or six against two."

The musicians had begun to pack their instruments. The young men turned silent and rose to their feet. Taking their sweet time, they ambled toward our table. Gustavo grabbed your forearm and squeezed hard. "Eduardo," he whispered, "as of this moment you're Mexican—*me oyes?* If they find out you're a gabacho, *estamos chingados.*" We're fucked.

The locals spread out in a fan, forming a semicircle around us. They appeared to be a few years older, around twenty, wearing blue jeans, pressed white guayaberas and cowboy boots. As they stood there, we saw our waitress flee to the kitchen. All at once the room seemed vast.

One, the tallest, stepped forward. *"De dónde son pues?"* he asked us, So where are you from? A dare or challenge, not a question. As he spoke, he pulled a long, black switchblade from the rear pocket of his jeans.

"De Saltillo," Zanahorio answered calmly.

"Y cómo te llamas, güey?" And what's your name, fucker?

"Felipe Madero," Gustavo replied without a pause, using his brother-in-law's name. One of them, who had also drawn a knife, caught his breath: "*Híjole,*" Shit. Letting that powerful name sink into their minds, your friend remained silent for a moment. "But everyone calls me Zanahorio," he added with a smile, relieving some of their alarm. Two or three of those young men tried to chuckle.

"*Y tú?*" the leader inquired, facing you. He cracked his knuckles. On the fingers he wore fat silver rings.

After uncountable heartbeats you answered, "Gustavo Dávila Ortega." By using his full, resonant name, you transformed yourself not just into a Mexican but into Zanahorio himself. He nudged your leg with a knee. "But you can call me Colacho," you finished, attempting a smile.

Most of the tension snapped: they broke out laughing, slapped each other's shoulders, offered us handshakes and *abrazos.* "Chingada madre," Motherfucker, some were saying, "we thought you were gringos—you had us fooled for a while. Sorry if we gave you a scare. Let's go find a place that's still open and we'll buy the drinks."

You can't recall what else they said, what we told them later, because it all passed like a bad dream. You do remember that they took us to a nightclub, where a man was singing while a woman performed a striptease with a python wrapped around her fluid body. It must have been very sensual. But you were concentrating so much on your speech that you barely noticed. That night you spoke the best Spanish of your life.

The Orizabans were all scions of important families. The father of one headed the Cuauhtémoc brewery, another was the mayor's son. They were all *hijos de papá,* daddies' boys, *niños popof* in the ephemeral patois of the time. They flashed bills in larger denominations than you had ever seen: 1,000, 10,000 pesos. They passed around cigarettes, "blond" American brands like Winstons and Raleighs, not the cheap, dark tobacco like Faros and Delicados smoked by most Mexicans. They refused to let us pay for a single beer or cocktail. One of them, who fancied himself a singer, took the microphone after the striptease and dedicated a song to "our brothers from Saltillo," with an effusive affection that would have been maudlin at home.

When the club closed its doors, the young men escorted us to our boardinghouse. "You're sleeping in this *pocilga*, this sty?" they asked. "We could have found you a better place." We agreed to gather in the zócalo at one o'clock the next afternoon, when they would show us the town.

But we would not see them again. After Gustavo had gulped his daily breakfast of three raw eggs in a glass, we cleared out of the city. We did not want the Orizabans to learn that one of their new friends was not from Saltillo but even farther north.

We hitched a ride on the back of an open truck. As the tropical air blew in our hair, you showed Zanahorio the black-and-blue mark where he had seized your arm.

"Colacho, that was close."

"At least it improved my Spanish."

"Híjole, know how cheap life can be in a place like this?"

Seeing Gustavo's grave expression, last night's fear returned in a rush. Before you could respond, he poked your sore arm, smiling. "Colacho, *No te agüites*," he said in argot, Don't melt, don't fall apart on me. We both laughed about the whole thing, feeling a surge of freedom with the wind in our face, wondering what the next town might bring us in those days so full of future.

The driver dropped us in the whitewashed main square of Veracruz with its graceful palm trees and white arches. From there we walked to the beach, took off our clothes and went swimming in our underwear, riding the soft breakers.

You had already taught Gustavo to body-surf in Mazatlán, where the waves were so buoyant that you could ride them with chest and shoulders out of water. In the late summer of 1960, on the beaches in the Gulf of Campeche, people had never seen such a strange sport. We showed some of the boys how to catch small waves while the girls watched from a distance, snickering at our shorts—not very pristine after weeks on the road.

We ate fresh shrimp with cold beer in the palm-roofed huts elevated on stilts at the shoreline. We fell asleep on the coarse brown sand. The next day on the beach Gustavo met a woman from Canada who invited him to her hotel. He spent the night there while you slept on the sand. At dawn he came to say that the lady had asked him to travel with her to Mexico City. By the logic of our unspoken rule we must separate.

"Don't worry, Colacho. We'll meet again."

"*Si Dios quiere,*" God willing, you whispered to yourself, by this time thinking like a Mexican.

We embraced and said goodbye. You sat on the beach, solo, watching the first light crack over the Gulf. Everything seemed upside down, backwards. You were used to Pacific beaches facing west, where the sun dropped instead of rising from the sea; you had grown accustomed to traveling with a friend, not being by yourself. Zanahorio had guided you across his country with camaraderie, a spirit of adventure, the savvy of a native, an insider. He had always been there for the *quite*, like a bullfighter who rescues another torero from danger. You would miss Gustavo deeply. At the same time, you knew now, you had grown to depend too much on him.

Sitting alone on the sand, the world began to look clearer. A copper sun emerged at the horizon, gleaming on the water, turning yellow as a yolk. Its light warmed your skin, your chest, arms, legs. Waves lapped the shoreline. You recalled a day on another beach long ago, where you watched a girl running over the sand, when desire stirred in your body for the first time.

Summer had ended. In a few days you would go home to California to start college. *Quién sabe,* Who knows when you would come back? It might be a long time: other cities, countries and continents called from farther away. Did you suspect the coming journey would take you beyond that sun, across Columbus's ocean? In a small way you discovered your New World in Mexico as surely as the explorer had encountered his, nearly five hundred years ago, on a sea like the one that shimmered in front of you. Here you found a people, their religion, their language; women, death, the body. Nobody could ever take that away. Whether you returned or not, it would all stay inside. *Ay México.*

Part Two

Old World

6. Galicia

As you stood on the deck, a black squall blew rain in your face. Could that gloomy coast off the bow be Spain, the land of sun, gardens, bullfights, beaches, wines? It looked more like northern Europe, even Scandinavia, perhaps Norway: inlets between somber cliffs, black promontories, a dark sea, low-hanging clouds and fog. The air felt colder than New York, where you had embarked on a freighter, and wetter than London, where you had boarded this steamer. You would learn soon that there are many Spains. Galicia was only one of them, as distinct from the rest of the country as Ireland from England.

Our ship entered the bay of Vigo, a grey and white city facing the Atlantic, sitting among green hills. Over the harbor flew the scarlet and yellow Spanish flag—blood and pus, the enemies of Generalissimo Francisco Franco called it, remembering the victims of the nation's Civil War. The dictator had been born here in Galicia, a Celtic region noted for fish and shellfish, crafty politicians, poverty, pilgrims, superstition and a melancholy older than the mist soaking us to our bones.

In their hooded oilskins the stevedores tied our steamer to the dock. They shouted to each other in *gallego,* a language close to Portuguese. Vigo did not look like Spain, the people did not speak Spanish, and it was too cold to be Spain.

After going through customs, you found a shop to buy winter clothes. You had not bothered to pack a coat, hat or gloves—just a ragged sweater—assuming the weather would be mild as in Los Angeles. You did not know that Spain's mostly a high country where it could be very, very cold.

The next morning dawned fair. You decided to do what any young Californian might do on such a promising day: go to the nearest beach. The air still felt cool but the sun shone brightly. The sky was cloudless above a cobalt sea. For years you had dreamed of swimming in the Atlantic Ocean.

An old tram wobbled south to Playa Samil, where pine trees grew almost to the shore. You saw nobody on the beach, not even an English, German or Swedish tourist fleeing from the northern fall and winter. Happy to be on the Continent at last, you lay down on the white sand, recalling sunny days on the beach at home and in Mexico. After a few minutes you stripped down to a pair of swimming trunks, sprinted to the water and took a running dive.

At once you knew why the beach was empty: the water was icy, cold as the Alaskan currents off the Pacific Northwest. Trying to warm up by staying in motion, you swam farther from shore. When a large roller swelled outside, you paddled to catch it and pushed off, suddenly your body cramped from your neck to your feet, the wave broke and pounded, flipped you over and over, down into darkness. Then you were waking, lying on hard sand in the backwash, your muscles taut, limbs blue and trembling, head throbbing. On your forehead you felt a raw bump, stinging from the saltwater. When you rose on your elbows, you saw a pair of bloodied legs and feet, as though they belonged to another person.

The breaker must have thrown you to the bottom, where your head hit the sand, maybe a rock, and carried you like a piece of driftwood to the shore, scraping over stones. In years of body-surfing up and down the Pacific coast from Big Sur to the Gulf of Tehuantepec, you had not been smashed by a wave or hurt like this. You had heard of culture shock but this was more—a knockout. You stared across Columbus's sea, feeling alone, wishing you had never come to this Old World. Wind gusted off the Atlantic, the cutting wind of November 2, 1964.

That was All Souls' Day, *Día de los Muertos*, Day of the Dead in Spanish-speaking countries. Later you would learn that the dull little port of Vigo had also been the first Spanish city seen by Ernest Hemingway, James Michener and Barnaby Conrad—all American authors who had written about Spain—because it lay on the Atlantic sea lanes. For you it will always bring to mind the day you nearly joined the souls of the departed.

In a daze you took the tram to the city, where an illuminated green cross led you to a pharmacy. Unlike American drug stores, spacious as supermarkets, where they sell anything from medicine to beach balls, this store was no bigger than a hotel room, sanitary as a hospital and smelled like one.

You were greeted by a middle-aged pharmacist in a starched white tunic. When he spotted your bloodied forehead, he walked around the counter, sat you in a chair and inspected the wound.

"*Joven,*" Young man, he announced pointing to your brow, "that's going to turn every color of the rainbow. How did it happen?"

"Oh I tried to ride a wave."

"You couldn't catch me dead in the ocean this time of year." He picked up a first aid kit, removed some cotton balls and a phial of alcohol, cleaned the bruise and doused it with pure iodine. Mercurochrome was not favored in Franco's Spain. The pharmacist's tone informed you, *entre hombres*, between men, that you were supposed to feel the burn. He dressed the wound with gauze and a large bandage.

Stepping back to examine his work, the man inquired, "When did you arrive in Spain, joven?"

"Yesterday."

"*Pues bienvenido.* A student trip, tourism or . . . adventure?" He gave you a complicit smile.

"I hope to travel for a while before finding a job."

"What sort of job?"

"Teaching English."

"You won't find any work like that here," he said, rubbing his bald, shiny head. "Maybe in Santiago de Compostela where there are so many students, or *las grandes capitales,* the big cities like Burgos or Madrid. *Suerte,"* Good luck.

"Thank you. How much do I owe?"

"*Nada,* joven." When you insisted on paying like a good American, for whom business must be business, the man repeated, "Nada, nada, nada." No word in any language conveys nothingness with more finality. The pharmacist straightened and ended, "Just tell your friends in America there are a lot of good people in Spain."

His words were loaded with patriotism and an implied defense of the regime. In order to avoid a political exchange with a man who had treated your wound for nothing, you asked, "How did you know I'm American?"

"Most of the movies we see are from *Holeegú,"* the pharmacist replied, making Hollywood sound like a town in the Punjab. "Also you have a slight accent. But don't get me wrong—your Castilian is quite good." You might have tricked the young men of Orizaba. It would be harder to fool the Spaniards.

Everything in Vigo seemed different. On the hilly streets you observed faces full of age and character, blasted by suffering—cripples dragging themselves on crutches, blind men who tapped down crooked alleys, priests crossing squares in windblown tunics, pale-faced nuns walking arm in arm, women sweeping the pavement in dressing gowns, girls in white skirts as stiff as lampshades, mothers who lowered their children's pants in broad daylight, letting them pee on the ground.

Mostly women and girls: where were all the men? Hundreds of thousands had been killed in the Civil War, thousands more were at sea with Europe's largest fishing fleet, still more had fled in search of jobs to Britain, France, Belgium, Holland, Denmark, Germany. For centuries the Galicians had been émigrés. In Mexico all Spaniards were called gallegos, no matter where they were born. The poet Rosalía de Castro spoke of the women as *"viudas de vivos e mortos"* in the region's melodious language, widows of the living and the dead.

Where were the ravishing ladies with carnations in their hair, peeking with black eyes over a fluttering fan, who appeared in books, movies and operas set in Spain? Where were Bizet's Carmen, Goya's *Maja*, the flamenco dancers, the Gypsies, the Lola Flores? In Vigo most of the women looked old, weary, dressed in black, their grey or white hair covered by a scarf or pulled tight in a yellowish bun, innocent of soap and water. Young girls looked wan and sickly, following their mothers around like shadows, their heads lowered in silence, tamely holding a shopping bag or umbrella in their hands. Before long you would see another kind of Spanish woman.

You rode a bus the next morning in the rain to Compostela, your head still throbbing. Here the body of St. James, Santiago, the country's patron saint, was supposed to be buried. On the day when Americans were electing Lyndon Johnson as president, you saw the cathedral, built of golden stone, with bulbous domes and soaring towers, where pilgrims have come for centuries, as they have gone to Jerusalem and Rome. You watched those fatigued, soaked travelers, Spaniards and foreigners, arrive on foot in the Plaza del Obradoiro, one of the most graceful and welcoming squares in the world. While the pilgrims passed slowly, dragging their tired feet, their eyes fixed on the church, you recalled the sense of awe you had known when older players trudged to the locker room after a football game in high school, sweating and bloodied, their cleats clicking on the cement floor.

Those men and women labored up the wide steps of the cathedral, through the Portico of Glory to the nave, where they kneeled and prayed, some of them weeping. You wondered if any of your forebears from Spain or Italy had walked into this temple, like so many European men and women during a whole millennium. The pilgrims rose to their feet, approached the main altar, hugged the saint's silver statue. It looked more like a smiling Buddha than one of Christ's apostles or the feared *Santiago Matamoros*, the Moorslayer who had sparked the Reconquest. You envied those believers their faith and endurance. But you found it hard to believe that their sins would be pardoned, as the Church avowed, or that they would be rewarded in heaven for having reached this sanctuary. Feeling out of place, at once skeptical and unworthy, you circled the figure of St. James without giving him the customary embrace.

During three days in that city the sun did not emerge, mist swirled around the towers and it rained, rained, rained. You walked through the streets of Santiago de Compostela, under the colonnades carved with coats-of-arms, by monumental palaces and temples whose walls seeped tears onto the wet, shining cobblestones, and whose blocks of granite sprouted moss, weeds, flowers. You passed stores with sacred vestments in the windows, butcher shops where lambs, hares, geese, ducks and chickens were hanging upside down, expensive restaurants with scallops, mussels, goose barnacles, squid and octopus on display, student taverns where you ate *caldo gallego,* a cabbage soup cooked for hours with ham, potatoes and greens, washed down by purple Ribeiro wine to keep out the cold.

Compostela was an ancient city that had not changed at its core, where everything felt older, even the rain. Little by little you were being absorbed in time, by the drizzle and fog, the living stone, in a way you had not known in Mexico, where the past had been destroyed, or in America, where it never existed. Here people were grounded in the moment while immersed deeply in a history that seemed to envelop them, the place, the air they breathed. You sensed that nothing could be grasped without this other dimension, these roots of time, this past in the present. You wanted to learn more about it, explore the country and see how they lived in the rest of Spain, this Old World, as if your own life somehow depended on it. You did not have a friend, not even a name or number on a scrap of paper, but you were young and free, and you were not alone.

Santiago de Compostela. JOAN MYERS

7. Castilla

The English traveler Richard Ford described the "bullfights, bandits and black eyes" of Romantic Spain. No matter how much the country has evolved since he wrote those words in the nineteenth century, foreigners have expected roughly the same on their first trip. In your case the bullfights were nothing new, though there was more afición in Spain, where the animals were larger and fiercer than in Mexico. As for the bandits they had left the mountains and moved into the councils of Franco's government. The black eyes would come soon enough.

On the surface fascist Spain was a masculine world. A married woman could not apply for a job, open a bank account, bring a lawsuit or travel on a train without her husband's permission, the dreaded *permiso marital*. Yet in many ways the nation was even more matriarchal than Mexico.

In parks, on buses and trains the young men pressed against their girlfriends, forcing embraces and kisses they could not have enjoyed in their cramped homes. Staring at the sky or trees, the women looked bored, indulgent with those tedious males, waiting for their real life and future: marriage and children. Their manifold charms, their dark lips, their eyes—black, brown, grey, green or blue—their spit-curls and earrings, their wide hips and ample breasts did not anticipate erotic intrigues, ardent raptures, endless swoons but a crib, a baby, *un hijo*. While they languished under the legal system, they ran the homes and the hearts of men.

You had been obscurely drawn to Spain by the country's women and your past: your Spanish great-great-grandmother, your mother's Mediterranean ancestors, southern California with its Hispanic peoples, aura and history. It was an instinct, felt but undefinable, an intimation of former life. You might compare it to the *querencia* of a fighting bull, the place in the arena where he's drawn by something: blood—his own, a man's, a horse's; a combination of light or shade, moisture or dryness, wind or calm and by what we'll never know. It's one of the most evocative and musical words in any language, rooted in the verb *querer*, to wish or love.

A man or woman can have more than one querencia or country, not merely on a map but in the mind and heart. Lawrence Durrell believed that one could claim "two birth-places . . . the place where you were born and . . . a place of predilection where you really wake up to reality." And might a person have even more querencias? For you there's America—mostly male; Mexico and Spain—largely female. These nations may seem patriarchal and machista, yet the deeper you go inside, the more you find the feminine.

At the outset you were not fortunate with Spanish women, who were just as guarded as the Mexican. You had little money and nobody like Zanahorio to guide you. Anyway the sort of sexual initiation you had undergone in Mexico could occur only once. A more subtle womanly favor would touch you in Spain.

From Galicia you took a bus to León, following the route of Christians who slowly wrested this land from Moors 1,100 years ago, fighting for every inch of territory. The city had been the seat of a medieval kingdom in northern Spain, so cold that a poet has called it "the capital of winter." Snowflakes floated from the milky sky as your bus pulled into the station.

After checking in at a hotel, you gave your torn, dirty sweater to a maid for laundering. By the next afternoon the garment had been cleaned and folded neatly on the bed with a small card: *"Zurcido por las Hermanas de la Concepción,"* Mended by the Sisters of La Concepción. (You remembered your old friend in Los Angeles who had taught you so much, now dumbly aware that he had been named for the Immaculate Conception.) Your room number and the date were penned in a delicate hand, unmistakably Spanish with crucified

7s, open-roofed 4s and winged 1s. At the desk they informed you that the nuns' order, Las Hermanas Franciscanas de la Concepción, eked out a livelihood by doing these small tasks for the hotel's clients. There was no charge for the mending, but one could leave a donation. "*Son muy pobres,*" the clerk said about them, Very poor. Imagining the pale hands of the sister who had repaired the sweater, you placed a 100-peseta bill in an envelope, feeling like the shoemaker of the fairy tale, watched over by a silent, invisible helper—not male elves but a female.

Many of the nuns and monks were indeed invisible, cloistered, like the Poor Clares and Carthusians. Others walked the streets in the habit of their order—Dominicans, Carmelites, Franciscans, Brothers of Mercy, Sisters of Charity. Spain had more religious than any other country in the world. You saw priests as well, monsignors, deans, canons, sextons, chaplains, seminarians, all attired in motley robes, cassocks, cloaks, scapulars adorned with emblems and insignias in diverse styles and colors. Like anyone else they went about their business. Raised in California where religion had declined or lost its sanctity, accustomed to Mexico where clergy could not wear vestments in public, you were fascinated by this hierarchical tableau in the midst of everyday life.

The doors of most churches, cathedrals and basilicas stood open. Although some were similar to those of Mexico in their profusion of images, they normally had fewer Virgins, more saints and Christs with wounds of clotted blood. There you had taken refuge from the heat, here you escaped from the rain and snow. Yet it was often colder inside than under the open sky: the breath of parishioners made little white clouds while they prayed, recited the rosary or crossed the transept. As in Mexico there were far more women than men. Sometimes you found yourself surrounded by females, old and young, most dressed in mourning. O Spanish churches, ladies in black, bald floors of frozen stone, unheated or barely warmed by a brazier with glowing embers.

Here too mendicants stood on the steps or in the plaza, asking for alms. An ordinance forbade it, but there's a trick to beat every law, a Castilian proverb says. And why should begging have been banned? It helped the poor to survive, others to have a good conscience. For a couple of *perras gordas,* "fat bitches" as the 10-*céntimo* pieces were called, each worth less than two-thousandths of a penny, you could be rewarded by God: *"Que Dios se lo pague,"* those souls recited when you placed coins in their open hands.

Like other Americans in Europe on their first stay, you were struck by the churches and cathedrals. Our country's story is the tale of peoples who have forsaken their traditions, like your Sicilian ancestors; those sanctuaries, bones of history, showed what they had lost. They had sheared their roots or failed to feed them, ignoring their native languages and customs in their zeal to melt into America's roiling pot of plenty. At the same time those temples recalled what the emigrants had fled. In almost every nation, in every age, the Vatican had connived with rulers and their engines of oppression. You could feel its weight and power in Spain, where *Iglesia y Estado,* Church and State, Catholicism and Falangism were the columns of Franco's regime, side by side with the Army.

The government and clergy enforced a suffocating morality. At times you had to flee the musty, asphyxiating air of churches, whose atmosphere was captured by a Spanish writer in these images: "the gloom of sacristies . . . the sense of guilt . . . the fear of human bodies." You sensed the prudery when you tried to approach young women, when you passed them on the street and they averted their eyes, when their mothers shielded them from the gaze of errant males. You remembered Mexico and the implacable fortress of female virginity.

Women in Spain could not enter a place of worship in pants or without a veil. They could be arrested for wearing a two-piece bathing suit on the beach or a one-piece bathing suit away from the beach, "its natural destiny" according to decree. It goes without saying that contraceptives and abortions were outlawed. Confessors told girls that if they had carnal relations before marriage, they would commit a sin, be abandoned by their boyfriends and never find another suitor. Young women lived in mortal fear of pregnancy; a single mother could be the ruin of her family. Girls took it for granted, even encouraged their fiancés to visit brothels, because they had been taught that men have more urgent desires than women: "That's the way they are, *los hombres.*" While the Second Republic had forbidden prostitution, Franco's ministers repealed the law, condoning sexual commerce in the face of their pious ideology. Pressures from the Church eventually drove the state to end its official support. Yet bordellos continued to operate in most cities, quietly tolerated. Hoping to find the feminine in other ways, you stayed away from them.

From León you traveled along the old Camino de Santiago to the city of Burgos. After checking into a *pensión*, you strolled across a bridge spanning the milky-green Arlanzón River, where a turreted gate housed niches for statues of the Cid, Count Fernán González and other Castilian heroes. When a local bus stopped nearby for passengers, through its frosty window you sighted a young woman's face fringed by chestnut hair. For some reason you grinned at her. She noticed, blushed, lowered her eyes, raised them and broke into a glorious smile. On that bright, cold afternoon beneath a cloudless sky, wide enough to hold the world, you were brushed by grace once more, maybe as Tom Sawyer was touched by the sight of Becky Thatcher, the Cid himself by Doña Ximena? But these males from life and books had not sighted a girl on a passing bus, and they would visit their loves many times. You would not see her again. Neither would you watch her become an old woman dressed in black. You will never meet her or even know her name, but the moment will blaze in your memory always.

Burgos had been Franco's headquarters during the war. In that city and others you saw the wreckage: bullet-pocked buildings, empty bunkers, maimed veterans, women and men in mourning. Plaster peeled from walls, curtains were threadbare, coats worn to a shine. We are speaking of a pervasive seediness, of lye-bitten, dirty streets, the smell of urine, rancid olive oil and barrel wine, dingy, dilapidated houses where the sun never reached. Yet some stores, hotels and *pensiones* were spotless because the women who worked there—always the women—kept them that way.

The W.C.'s rivaled the forbidding toilets of Mexico: open stalls above black pits, where you placed your feet on shoe-shaped ceramic treads; pissoirs with 25-watt light bulbs, so cold that urine steamed against the porcelain bowls; wooden corrals on trains, where freezing wind sliced through the slats of third-class carriages while you tried to relieve yourself. Instead of the bland American "Men" and "Women," Castilian rhetoric styled latrines *"Caballeros"* and *"Damas,"* Gentlemen and Ladies, as if Don Quixote himself had named them in his fevered brain. But they did not smell quite gentlemanly or ladylike. Sometimes you had to hold your breath or pinch your nose to avoid the stench. If you needed running water and toilet tissue softer than sandpaper, you had to enter a restaurant or hotel where an older lady in a black-and-white uniform handed you a washcloth, starched and ironed, for a 5-peseta tip. (You recalled the old women in Mexican bordellos who offered towels and other tokens to customers.)

Poverty sharpened the edge of ordinary life. But Spaniards did not lose their taste for whiling away the hours, *pasando el rato,* as the saying goes. You had never seen a people in such a hurry to do nothing. For them leisure actually meant doing something, *algo,* while work meant doing nothing, nada. Their real life was not a job, which many confessed to hating, but the freedom not to work, to do what they pleased, drink their coffee or wine, read the paper, watch pedestrians go by. When they tipped glasses in their favorite toast—*"Salud, pesetas y tiempo para gastarlas!"*—Health, money and time to spend it!—the most important thing was the last, time. They were teaching you how to value it, how to use it for precious nothing, to live right here, where there is only now. The ever-present cry of lottery vendors on the streets of Spanish cities, those blind men with their strident nasal twang like some voice of destiny, reminded you to seize the instant, the hour, the day. *"Tiras para hóoy . . . Para hóoy . . . Hóoy!"* Tickets for todaay! . . . For todaay! . . . Todaay!

People took their leisure seriously. When you reached Madrid, you encountered men and women who were willing to ride a bus or train across town in order to have a cup of coffee at a bar where they liked the roast and blend. They spoke of taking *"mi café," my* coffee, as though it were exclusively theirs, unlike every other in that bar, in the town or the wide world. For them in fact their café and their city were the world, the otherworld too. As the song says, *"De Madrid al cielo,"* Where can one go from Madrid but to heaven?

In late November you found a tiny apartment near the Puerta del Sol, Door of the Sun, the pounding heart of the capital and the country. Within a few days you had secured a job as an English tutor for Spanish students. We met in a bar or café for lessons since the company's office was a mere hole-in-the-wall on a sunless alley in the old town.

One of the first students, Rodrigo Serna, soon broke his contract and struck a deal with you. In exchange for an hour of tutoring every weekday, he would show you around the city. He loved the old quarters where he could dine in the *fondas, ventas, bodegas* and *mesones,* various types of traditional taverns or inns. Before the tourist boom would start a few years later, Rodrigo foresaw that a knowledge of English could be useful in the new Spain. He still took courses at the Universidad Complutense, but he made a living as a food critic for magazines, newspapers and a radio station. He was an example of the *pluriempleo* or multiple jobs that so many Spaniards held down.

Rodrigo was twenty-nine and single, young enough to be free of family life, old enough to be a guide or an elder brother. On both his mother's and father's side your new friend belonged to a venerable line of journalists, writers, scholars and politicians. He had a long, aristocratic nose, clear green eyes and an insatiable appetite for good eating and drinking.

Although countless Spaniards were impoverished, Rodrigo taught you that they had not forgotten how to live, to take pleasure.

Families often spent more on food and wine than on clothes or housing, he told you. Many people, rich and poor, ate fresher meals in more abundance than most Americans, not to mention the wine they drank at a time when it was a frill or luxury in the U.S. and other countries.

You often joined Rodrigo for an hour of English and a light breakfast, usually a *café con leche* with bread, a roll or croissant. Other days we would meet at mid-morning for an apéritif and *tapas*, a word that still had not entered the global lexicon: hors d'oeuvres made from peppers, artichokes, potatoes, cheese, olives, mushrooms, one or more of them skewered on a toothpick to become a *pincho*; small fish like sardines or anchovies, shellfish like shrimp, clams, mussels, goose barnacles, squid, octopus; snails; *jamón serrano*, air-cured ham; sausages like chorizo and *morcilla*, blood pudding; *tortilla*, Spanish omelette; empanadas, croquettes. Each of these morsels was prepared in an astonishing diversity of simple or complex, local and regional ways.

If Rodrigo found himself between jobs, he would invite you to lunch, when stores, offices and schools closed for the principal meal of the day, *la comida*. The nation ground to a stop. By three o'clock the streets looked as if they had been emptied by the threat of a bomb raid.

In one of the taverns, restaurants or inns on the narrow streets around the Plaza Mayor, we would begin with a first course like soup, lentils, *olla podrida*, stew; cooked vegetables or the ubiquitous tortilla. The opener would be followed by a second course of fish, a third of meat or fowl, sometimes with a salad on the side; fruit and coffee: all of it washed down by the wine of the country, nearly as cheap as mineral water in those days. If it was a Wednesday in Madrid, the customary day for *cocido madrileño*, we ordered this hodgepodge cooked with onions, garlic, beef, ham, chickpeas, potatoes, carrots, cabbage and noodles—a first, second and third course all in one.

When we had time, we would order a cognac and dessert: the inevitable *flan* in many variations; rice pudding spiced with cinnamon, anisette or brandy; *natillas*, a soft custard; *cuajada*, a curdled pudding; stuffed fried pastries called *bartolillos*; diverse sweets, cakes and tarts. Or we would stroll through the twisting lanes of Hapsburg Madrid in search of pastry shops. There we would buy sweetmeats with names that alluded to their conventual origins, Rodrigo explained: *yemas de Santa Teresa*, St. Teresa's candied egg yolks; nun's delights, *bocadillos de monja*; saint's bones, *huesos de santo*; candied egg yolks in almond rolls, orange-and-almond cake first brought to convents by Jewish *conversas*; St. James's cake, *tarta de Santiago*, topped with the apostle's red cross. Or we would stop at one of the glassy, modern cafés near the Plaza de Callao and order the ultimate in divine decadence, *tocino del cielo*, "pork fat from heaven," concocted of whole eggs, additional yolks, plain and caramelized sugar, a dessert so rich that it might induce a sublime siesta or an ascent to Kingdom Come. One could choose a lighter treat like *pedos de monja*, nun's farts, pastries that also inspired levitation into the celestial sphere.

At better restaurants we would linger over the satisfactions of the *sobremesa*, remaining at table to drink, smoke, converse and delay as long as possible the return to work. "Spain is one of the world's last paradises for eating and drinking," Rodrigo declared one day while he leaned back in his chair and blew a cloud of bluish smoke from his Havana cigar. "And for afterwards too."

"That's right because the drinking doesn't stop during the sobremesa."

"*Nunca,*" Never.

In restaurants, hotels, pensiones or boardinghouses, homes humble or magnificent, everywhere the Spanish lunch worked on the python's principle: gorging followed by lethargy and repose. Perhaps for this reason the people wished each other "*Buen provecho*" or said "*Que le aproveche*" before each meal, the equivalent of "*Bon appétit*" but with more emphasis on nourishment and digestion. Few among the rich or poor could resist a siesta after the bountiful mid-afternoon repast.

When businesses reopened at four or five o'clock, people might take coffee or tea, perhaps with a pastry to begin the second half of the lengthy Spanish *jornada*, split in two by the Great Divide of the sacred midday meal. Now children were walking back to school, wielding foot-long *bocadillos*, veritable boats of hard-crusted bread relieved by a few slices of chorizo, cheese or the unavoidable tortilla. In the coming hours, as dusk approached, bars began to fill again—more drinks, more tapas, more conversation—and the whole thing started over. When suppertime rolled around, it was ten or eleven o'clock.

Rodrigo did not accompany you for the last meal of the day. He spent evenings with his fiancée, whom you never had a chance to meet. Nor did you see his parent's flat in the patrician Salamanca quarter of Madrid, where he continued to live. Like so many Spaniards he separated his personal and public lives in a way that would have been considered odd in America.

"*Sabes*, Rodrigo," you told him one day during an extended sobremesa, "in my country most young men your age have already moved out of their parents' house. A lot of women too."

"*Hombre*, you can afford to do that in America. Here it's very hard for a man to marry or leave home in his twenties—we need to save our money to buy an apartment and it takes years to find one. *Coño*, that's how my girlfriend and I spend our weekends. There's a real shortage of housing in Madrid and lots of other cities." Rodrigo noticed the empty carafe on our table and summoned the waiter, "*Camarero!*"

"Do parents mind if their kids stay at home?"

He laughed. "Are you kidding? They love it. Pues maybe not so much my father but my mother would be happy if I stayed forever. And I wouldn't mind it either if I didn't have a girlfriend because *mamá's* cooking is—" Rodrigo completed his sentence with the classic gesture of praise, curling the thumb and fingers of his right hand in front of his mouth, then releasing them into the air with the sound of a kiss. "What about you, Eduardo, do you miss your family?"

"Yes but it's good to be on my own."

Our waiter served a new carafe of red wine. Rodrigo, who relished being our *escanciador* or wine steward, poured us two more glasses of *tinto*.

"I can't imagine being so far away from home," he said. "Do you think you'd like to live in Spain, I mean for good?"

"I need to see more of the country—I've only been here about six weeks. But if I had to decide at this moment, I'd say yes. By the way, Rodrigo, I've never told you that one of my great-great-grandmothers was Spanish."

He smiled, raising his glass for a toast. "That means we're brothers, Eduardo. Where was she from?"

"All we know is that she married a German from Dresden, lived there, had three sons and died of tuberculosis in her 30s. One of those sons emigrated to the U.S.—my great-grandfather."

"So you have reasons of blood to be here. What do you like most about Spain?"

"Hard to put in words. There's something about the sense of time, the way you manage to live for the moment even though the past is always here. It's like another dimension—it makes me feel less alone than in America, where everything's sort of temporary and you're always on your own."

"I'm not sure I grasp what you mean, Eduardo. Here the past can be a burden."

"I see that in the way many Spaniards still haven't gotten over the Civil War. But as a foreigner I'm free of those memories."

"So it's an artificial freedom that's not available to us." Your friend called the waiter again, telling him to bring the house's box of *puros*, cigars.

"Maybe it would be artificial for you, Rodrigo, not for me. And living in a foreign country is the best way to understand your own."

"Nietzsche said that a long time ago."

"Right. And leaving home's the only way I'll ever know if I want to live abroad someday." Holding up your *chato* of red wine, the traditional, small glass used in Spanish taverns, bars and inns, you toasted: "*A España.*"

When Rodrigo raised his glass, a shapely Spanish woman strode by, almost brushing our table with her swaying hips.

"*A las españolas,*" To Spanish women, Rodrigo said, following the lady with his eyes until she disappeared in another room. "That reminds me, Eduardo. Do you ever go *de putas*—whoring?"

"I had my share of that in Mexico. I'm looking for something better now. Sabes, Madrid has a kind of coarse, erotic air about it, unlike any other city I know."

"So what do you think of las españolas?"

"I hardly know them."

"Our women don't have the means to turn themselves out like the French or Italians. But"—Rodrigo composed his next phrase with quotation marks made by two fingers of each hand—'*saben estar*'—they know how to be themselves, how to live in their own skin, how to create a presence. Like that *morena* who just walked by."

Our waiter returned bearing a large wooden humidor. He opened it and displayed two drawers lined in green felt, one for Cubans, one for domestic cigars from the Canary Islands. We chose a pair of *habanos,* slim coronas with a band saying "El Rey del Mundo." The waiter set a steel cigar-cutter and a box of cedar matches on our table. He closed the humidor. "*Que disfruten, Señores,*" he said, May you enjoy, gentlemen.

Rodrigo prepared his postprandial puro, feeling of the golden leaf, slicing off the tip and joking about circumcision, warming the end with one match, lighting it with another. He blew smoke into the air that was already dense with the fumes from other diners, nearly all men, seated at tables in the dark, wood-paneled mesón.

He took a long draw from his puro. "*A propósito,* Eduardo, do you know how one of our writers described death?" Rodrigo did not wait for an answer. "A state in which one can no longer smoke habanos." We both laughed for a full five seconds. Only in Spain did you send forth peals like that. You didn't realize this at the time because you were immersed in the place and moment.

Rodrigo looked as though he were trying to remember something. "Eduardo," he started finally, "I was thinking about something a character says in one of Hemingway's books."

"Which one?"

"*Fiesta*, his most Spanish novel."

"It's called *The Sun Also Rises* in English."

"I prefer our title. Anyway do you remember when Jake Barnes says more or less, 'What matters is not understanding what the world's all about, but learning how to live in it'? I often recall those words during the sobremesa, which by the way is one of the most civilized customs in the world."

"*De acuerdo.* I enjoy these ceremonies of daily life in Spain like eating, drinking, smoking and almost everything else I've seen so far. It's as if you're not alone because tradition and the past are always behind you."

Drawing deeply on his habano, Rodrigo said, "Spanish life is like a movie from the golden age of cinema when tobacco—cigarettes or cigars—appears over and over again. Their presence and their smoke are the spirit that holds the characters and scenes together."

Without giving you the time to respond, Rodrigo was already thinking about the next stimulation of his taste buds. "Eduardo," he said, "we need a good snifter of warm brandy to accompany this Cuban." Turning toward the kitchen, he called, "Camarero!"

As we ate tapas and pinchos in a bar one afternoon, Rodrigo ended our English lesson in the usual way, shifting to Castilian. "Eduardo, *quiero llevarte a un sitio nuevo,*" I want to take you somewhere new.

Looking at your watch, you replied, "It's three-thirty and I'm starving. But isn't it a little late for lunch at a restaurant, even in Spain?"

"It's never too late where I'm taking you."

He guided you down the steep concrete steps from the Plaza Mayor onto the winding Calle de Cuchilleros, Street of the Knifesmiths. He stopped at number 17 on the left, where you saw a sign over the door of a building with Mudéjar brick and wood panelling: "Antigua Casa Sobrino de Botín."

"Eduardo, I'm going to invite you to lunch at the oldest restaurant in the world. Procope in Paris also makes that claim but they had to close their doors during the Revolution. Botín has been serving continuously since 1725."

"Coño!" you exclaimed like a Spaniard, making your friend burst into laughter.

When we passed the threshold, we were greeted by Antonio González, owner of Botín. The middle-aged gentleman escorted us to his private table in a corner on the ground floor. While he tended to other clients, a waiter served us narrow, tapered glasses of dry sherry and a plate of dark red, lightly-veined jamón serrano.

Rodrigo explained that his family were regulars at Botín. "Only Antonio's good friends are invited to eat at this table, Eduardo." He sipped from his glass. "The sherry and jamón are on the house."

"It's the best ham I've ever tasted."

"I'll tell you the story about it."

"I knew you would."

"It's called Jabugo from the name of a town in the mountains of Huelva. The most expensive jamón in all of Spain, made from the meat of the *cerdo ibérico*—the wild native pig who eats nothing except wild acorns. It's so much in demand that even a trusted buyer like Antonio has to pay for it in cash, months before it's delivered."

We set into a four-course meal centered around the house specialty of *cochinillo*, roast suckling pig. In between talking to guests, taking telephone calls and consulting with his staff, Antonio visited our table several times.

Your friend observed over the long sobremesa, "Antonio González is an artist whose art is running a mesón. Notice how graceful his movements are, how he never loses his composure, how he smiles in the midst of the inevitable crises that occur in a restaurant where nearly all tables are full the year around. He has the gift of performing these duties while appearing to be entirely at ease. Y a propósito, Hemingway ate here often and he was a good friend of Antonio's."

By the time we finished lunch, it was nearly six o'clock. A diner or two were still taking coffee or brandy. "Sabes," you told Rodrigo, "in America some people would already have finished supper by this time."

"*Qué barbaridad!* No offense, Eduardo, but you live in a country of savages."

The owner must have overheard because he drew close to us, saying, "Rodrigo, I do not mean to eavesdrop. But I believe our countrymen have been known to be as violent as Eduardo's."

"We weren't talking about that kind of savagery, Don Antonio," your friend explained. "We were just saying that Americans eat their meals much earlier than us—too early, in fact."

"*O, perdón,*" the host said. "Incidentally I love American food, especially the beef. Have you ever traveled to the U.S., Rodrigo?"

"No." For the first time your friend seemed to be caught without words.

We rose from our table, several pounds heavier and a lot happier. Holding each of us gently by the forearm, smiling, Antonio accompanied us to the door.

"*Volveré,*" you told him, I'll be back.

"You are always bienvenido, welcome here, Eduardo. Like Rodrigo and his family."

While Spaniards celebrated life through eating, drinking, smoking and talking, they went on paying tribute to mortality in their time-honored ways. Was it merely chance that led you to Spain after Mexico, another nation with a profound cult of death? And in particular to the Spanish heartland, where transience is almost palpable, more than in other parts of the Peninsula? With their clear, dry, fatal air, Castilla and Anáhuac are twin plateaus. In both places a cadaver is more alive than anywhere in the world, the Spanish poet Lorca said—before being murdered by fascists. (The quest for his corpse has continued for decades, exerting more influence by its absence than a living person.) You would learn soon what he meant.

In those years even a modest apartment building had a *portero*, a doorman who watched the entrance, screened visitors, handled mail, swept stairways and above all made the residents feel important. José Paniagua—his surname evoked the staffs of life, bread and water—held that position in your old building near the Puerta del Sol. From the age of six to twenty he had ridden a donkey, loaded with eight *arrobas* of milk (about two hundred pounds), from a dairy farm to the city of Sevilla, where he made door-to-door deliveries seven days a week. After marrying he migrated to Madrid in search of a better life, which for a Spaniard of his class often meant an easier job. Now José worked shorter hours, wore a uniform and occupied a free apartment. He lived with his wife and two grown children in the unheated, one-bedroom basement of our building, where sunlight had never been seen.

As soon as you returned home that night, you knew something was wrong. The main door had been wedged open, the carpet had been rolled back, the doorman's cubbyhole was dark. When you reached the landing, José's son spotted you from below, walked up the stairs from the basement and greeted you solemnly, "Buenas noches. *Mi padre ha fallecido,*" the young man stated in the formal manner, My father has deceased. Without thinking twice, you embraced him: "Hombre, I'm very sorry for you, for your mother and sister." Although you had only lived there a month, José and his family had already made you feel like a member of their small community.

"*Desea verle?*" he asked, Would you like to see him?

"*Claro que sí.*"

The young man led you downstairs to the windowless apartment lit by two yellow lightbulbs. José's widow sat in the lone chair of the living room-kitchen, distraught, surrounded by relatives and friends. Her son guided you to the other room, just big enough for two pieces of furniture—a double bed and a night stand—where his father's corpse lay in repose, attired in doorman's livery. Contemplating his face, rapt, his daughter sat by his side.

You stepped closer. The salt-and-pepper stubble of José's beard showed against his ashen countenance. Sockets of leathery skin surrounded his eyelids. To prevent his face from collapsing, a piece of gauze circled his head and jaw. His hands and feet were bound by strips of white cloth so that his limbs would not splay from rigor mortis. Folded on his stomach, José's hands held a crucifix. His bony fingers had yellowish nails, purple at the base, dirt beneath the tips. On his feet he wore the pointed black leather shoes that most Spanish men reserve for baptisms, first communions, weddings and burials, not excluding their own.

People arrived and departed, viewed José, spoke about him, consoled the family while some of the women prepared food. Around midnight a carpenter brought an austere coffin of pine that smelled of freshly cut wood. His assistant carried a large crucifix and a pair of brass candleholders about four feet tall. They lifted José into the box and placed the cross between the candles at his head. For a long time you stood observing him, longer than you had ever watched a corpse, side by side with the other guests. You made a silent peace with José and with death, who is always alive in Spain.

The family could not afford to embalm his cadaver. In any case they would not have surrendered José to an undertaker who would spirit him away to perform death's dirty work, disguising him as a waxen effigy. No. They allowed the man to lie in state at home where they were the ones in charge. For centuries this was how Spaniards bade farewell to their deceased. Death was not the end of a life, you realized now, but a part of it here. Not something to be cleansed, covered, beautified as in the funeral homes of the United States, but rather faced, confronted, accepted as José's survivors were facing it, feeling, living it. They would not sleep until he was buried. That's the meaning of a wake, to keep a vigil, *velar* in Spanish—to stay alert, be watchful, to contemplate a corpse in the midst of life.

On the second day his family buried José at sunrise. If they had waited longer, his cadaver would have putrefied. After returning to your apartment from the cemetery, changing clothes and going outside again, you saw the doorman's wife and daughter on their hands and knees at the main entrance, scrubbing the stairway. You noticed their hands, raw and red from washing steps, floors, windows, walls and dishes in ice-cold winter water.

A Castilian proverb claims, "It's best to be born in Italy, to live in France, to die in Spain." But if you've lived a whole life in poverty, if a family must return to their jobs on the same day a husband or father is buried, then it would be better to die in another country. Many, especially women, could not afford the luxury of free time: their toil sustained the leisure of the rest. While José's wife and daughter swabbed those steps, thousands of other poor people, *los pobres y humildes*, were rising from beds all over Spain, going to their joyless work.

Meanwhile a few others were leading their lives of privilege, driving cars, boats and airplanes, living in houses as good or better than their peers' in Great Britain, France, Germany or the U.S. Those wealthy Spaniards flaunted their fortunes as though they were grinding an ax. "Our side won the war," they seemed to be saying. "Swallow it, losers." They abused the poor with an impudence you had not seen anywhere.

Since Rodrigo spent weekends with his girlfriend and their families, you took advantage of those days to explore the region. At first you tried hitchhiking, as you had done in Mexico, where a compassion for the underdog prevailed. But Spain was too autocratic for such a liberal mode of travel. Few vehicles drove the highways. If cars appeared, they usually passed without stopping, even accelerating as if their owners feared a hitchhiker might contaminate them. The attitude of Spanish drivers seemed to be, If you can't afford to own an automobile or use public transportation, you don't deserve a ride. Some, naturally all men, tried to run you off the shoulder of the highway, sticking their head out the window as they sped by, yelling insults and making the sign of the cuckold with their index and little finger. The charity you had witnessed on the streets and in churches did not extend to the country's roads.

Since thumbing for a ride was slow and risky, you rode trains and buses from Madrid to the outlying towns, hamlets and villages. One day while you casually conversed with a man in a third-class carriage, two sergeants of the national police, the *Guardia Civil*, lumbered down the aisle. They wore heavy, green wool uniforms and three-cornered, patent-leather hats. When they glowered at us, we stopped speaking at once, as though they had struck us with a lightning bolt. In that second you felt a stab of fright that you had never known in your country. *La pareja*, "the pair" of guards sauntered away, silencing the other passengers with a mere glance. When they left our carriage, your companion whispered, "The difference between us is that I must stay and you will leave." Then you understood the meaning of fear without end.

Jokes offered citizens a medium for abiding the terror. In a hushed voice somebody would ask, "Have you heard the one about . . . ?" "Do you know why Franco did this or that?" One could argue that no person in the history of Spain has generated more jokes than the dour Caudillo, who reportedly smiled only three times in public during his reign of forty years. "The discrepancy between a stodgy, silent and joyless Franco," one writer remarked, "and the Spaniard who laughs his head off at anything, tells us something about the regime . . ."

One joke had the dictator and his wife traveling in their private airplane. "I'm going to throw a one-thousand peseta bill out the window to make a Spaniard happy," he told her. Señora Franco inquired, "Why don't you throw out two bills and make two people happy?" Before the Generalissimo could answer, the pilot turned to ask him, "Why don't you throw yourself out the window and make all of us happy?"

As you listened to jokes and retold them, you were learning more about the country's language and dialects, so different from

Mexico's. Many Spaniards spoke with pride, with a flavor for the apt word or idiom that had almost vanished in America. You met farmers, peasants and workers who expounded with the dignity of grand *señores*. They were embodiments of an oral culture that had endured for centuries. Like your old friend Concepción they uttered phrases that poets would fancy in English. You recall a man with a thousand wrinkles who declared with ancient serenity, watching the sun descend toward the horizon, *"La tarde aún tiene cara,"* The afternoon still has a face. There would be more sunlight that day.

Even younger Spaniards like Rodrigo, who belonged to the first generation brought up on television, took pleasure in a fitting proverb or turn of phrase. Of course for him they were largely related to his passion for the table. When you told him about the lumpy mattress of the bed in your apartment, he raised his glass, advising, "Eduardo, '*A mala cama, colchón de vino,*'" For a bad bed, a mattress of wine. When you considered ordering a rabbit stew for one of our lunches, Rodrigo smiled and declared, *"No comas conejo de fonda, ni te cases con mujer cachonda.* Translate that one for me." You tried but the adage lost all of its rhyme and most of its reason in English. Enough to say that many of your friend's culinary maxims related to sexuality, as in the well-known *"Uvas con queso saben a beso,"* Grapes with cheese taste sweet as a kiss, a cliché enhanced by Rodrigo's personal addendum, *"y con vino es un embeleso,"* and with wine it's bliss.

The Spaniards' linguistic imagination revealed itself notably in cursing and profanity. One afternoon at a soccer match in Madrid, you were seated behind a pair of twin brothers and their father. Those boys, who were not more than nine or ten years old, chanted for hours at the visiting team from the Canary Islands:

> *¡Tenerife es una mierda!*
> *¡Tenerife es una mierda!*

> Tenerife is a bunch of shits!
> Tenerife is a bunch of shits!

They alternated their favorite cheer with a theme and variations: *"Hijos de puta! Hideputas! Hijos de la Gran Puta! Hijos de la Gran Puta que los parió!"* Sons of whores! Whoresons! Sons of the Great Whore! Sons of the Great Whore who bore them! These were interspersed with exhortations for the enlightenment of the home team such as *"Dales en el culo! Pínchales los cojones!"* Kick their asses! Pinch them in the balls! The boys' father beamed with pride. He had raised two sons who spoke like men, who would have hair on their chest one day, as the saying goes in Spanish.

Accustomed to Mexico, where you can get killed for mentioning a person's mother, you were surprised to hear the Spaniards turn this taboo upside down. For them the idiom *"de puta madre,"* like a whore-mother, could be a supreme form of praise.

"How's the food there?" you might ask Rodrigo as we wandered by a restaurant.

"Se come de puta madre," You can eat there like a whore-mother, he responded, smacking his lips and pulling you inside.

Spaniards also invoked prostitutes to express their rage. *"Me cago en la puta!"* I shit on the whore! Rodrigo would shout if he was angry. In fact he and his compatriots appeared to be shitting frequently on others. Not just on prostitutes but the dead and all the saints too, even on God, the Virgin Mary and her poor mother. An incensed bus driver offered this posy for his admiring passengers one day in Valladolid: *"Me cago en los sangrientos calzones de la Virgen y en la puta que la parió!"* I shit in the bloody drawers of the Virgin and on the slut who bore her!—an exclamation with more theological complexity than whole volumes by the Church Fathers and with fatal consequences for the doctrine of the Immaculate Conception. Only a people with an intimate sense of the divine would be capable of such sacrilege.

Before long the avalanche of tourists would alter Spain for good. The country would become prosperous, eventually join the European Community and NATO. You had arrived in the nick of time, when life was cheap—one could live well on the equivalent of five or six dollars a day—when Spaniards still had not wearied of foreigners. They enjoyed talking and learning how we lived. Americans seemed novel to them, unlike travelers from other places, beings who had walked straight out of magazines, songs and movies. A woman on a bus to Segovia once asked you, *"Hay hombres calvos en los Estados Unidos?"* Are there bald men in America? *"Muy pocos, Señora,"* Very few, Madam, you replied, not wishing to destroy her illusion.

In the mid-1960s Spain persevered with many of its old ways. If you returned late to your hotel or pensión, you had to call a *sereno* or night watchman to open the main door. People clapped their palms in streets and squares to summon him. The sound of their call reverberated against the walls with a lingering intonation, *"Se—reée—no! . . . eé—no!"* Waiting for the man to arrive under the black and starry sky, what else could one do but converse with the other guests, also stranded yet in a good mood after being out on the town? The tradition was unnecessary but wholly convivial, like many in Spain.

As we shivered and rubbed our hands together, the watchman's voice came out of the night—*"Va!"* He's coming!—followed by the pounding of his wooden staff on the sidewalk. Between our claps and the sereno's tat-tat, we were communing in a nocturnal language not very different from the beating of drums in the rainforest. Next we would hear the jangling of keys as he approached along the deserted avenue. Silhouetted in the halo of light beneath a corner street lantern, our savior emerged from the darkness: the man who controlled the doors of the city until morning, the St. Peter of Spanish nights, wearing a cap and navy-blue uniform or a wool cloak the worse for wear. Since he had to spend so many lonely, late hours between calls, usually stopping in a local bar to avoid the cold—where else to stop in Spain?—he often arrived as soused as the rest of us. Alcoholism was the occupational hazard of serenos. Now everyone was in good spirits as the tipsy watchman fumbled through his enormous ring of keys like a medieval castellan, trying one after another in the lock, finally opening the door to the relief of his frozen clients. "Buenas noches," we told him with a sigh as we entered, offering one or two coins to the good soul, who would go back to the nearest bar and disburse them on the wine of the country.

Some believe those men were on the government dole, for who was more aware of where people stayed, when and with whom? If some serenos were indeed informers, they must have misled the police with fantastical stories from their sodden brains. Was it by coincidence that their calling disappeared shortly after the dictator's death? Or was it because the advent of intercoms and entry phones in small hotels and pensiones made watchmen obsolete?

Each generation believes it has seen more than the next. *"Todo tiempo pasado fue mejor,"* All times past were better, the poet said. Ours had the luck to know Spain when it preserved some usages unaltered for centuries. Wine-grapes continued to be pressed by foot at some vineyards in the 1960s, for example. Yet we missed by decades what older Spaniards had known. Serenos once called the watches of the night in addition to opening the doors of hotels: a custom that had given them their lovely name. *"Las dó-ce han dá-do y se-reée-no!"* they used to cry, Twelve o'clock and calm! Or *"Las tres han dá-do y nu-blá-do!"* Three o'clock and cloudy! and so on according to the weather. Like street-callers during the day—knife sharpeners, vegetable and fruit vendors—also subjects of popular traditions that survived tenuously—night watchmen had a peculiar tone for their long-drawn cry. Nobody who has listened to it could forget, old men and women said. Sometimes you imagine hearing it while you fall asleep, late at night or at dawn, the reassuring call from far away . . . *". . . y se-reée-no!"* Your ancestors from Spain could have listened to those words, you guessed.

Just as the profession of night watchmen has disappeared, others will follow. Soon there will be no more artisans who ply their age-less tools to shape *botas,* the supple leather bottles, lined with pitch, for storing wine and oil. Ambulant knife sharpeners will fade away like the plaintive sound of their whistles. So too will the makers of the earthenware jugs called *botijos,* whose clay sweats in hot weather, keeping the water inside cool but not cold, much tastier than iced or refrigerated.

Spaniards still argue about whether they lived a better life under Franco. The nation was poor and governed by a despot but graced by genial customs and ancient crafts, free of excessive traffic, crime, drugs, pollution, AIDS, unemployment, taxes, debt. So reactionaries claim, "We were better off under Franco." Their opponents, recalling the heroic struggle against the dictator yet disappointed with the new democracy, respond, "We were better off against Franco." The others, perhaps speaking for the rest, say, "We were younger under Franco." We were younger alright. *Ay España.*

8. Cataluña

As the long Christmas vacation approached, your students dispersed. You had saved a little to travel during the holidays. Although winter had arrived, the weather warmed as you rode a train across the Castilian plateau and the former kingdom of Aragón. In Cataluña, the northeastern corner of the Peninsula, you felt at home: the climate, countryside and vegetation reminded you of northern California. Mountains rose from the interior, fertile fields and valleys sloped to the sea, the coastline zigzagged with bays and coves. The people seemed less foreign than Castilians, less absorbed by God and death. They were more practical, industrious and modern—like Americans in some ways. As you would discover fast, they were also very different.

On Christmas Eve you reached Montserrat, the medieval monastery set on a promontory of cone-shaped rocks that recalled landscapes by Salvador Dalí, who was born nearby. It was a sacred site for Catalans, a symbol of their age-old independence. Because they opposed the illegal revolt against the Republic in 1936, Franco suppressed their language, traditions and culture ruthlessly. Yet in December of 1964 Montserrat may have been the freest spot in the Iberian Peninsula. As a concession to the Church the Generalissimo respected its sanctuary, the one place in the country where a regional language, in this case Catalan, could be spoken in public, chanted and sung in the liturgy.

At the midnight Mass on *Nochebuena*, the Good Night of the 24th, you listened to the service in that odd, clipped tongue. You understood little beyond the people's faith as we stood in line before the *Verge Bruna,* the *Moreneta,* The Dark One, patroness of Cataluña

93

(Catalunya for the locals), the Black Virgin with a Christ-child in her lap and a golden sphere of the world in her hand. Her cult had spread from this chapel across the seas to the whole Hispanic world, even as far as Tijuana, where the young mother Alfa worshiped her as a protector of women in childbirth. You had not mustered courage to embrace the statue of warlike Santiago, the Moorslayer and patron saint of Spain, but you joined the congregation of thousands to kiss the gentle lady's smooth, black face with reverence.

From the mountains you traveled by instinct to the sea. Following the route of the Republican retreat from Franco's advancing army, you headed north along the Costa Brava. The air was warmer than in Galicia, the water almost as cold. You walked on the deserted beaches instead of swimming. Every afternoon you ate fresh seafood, drank the wine of the country and *cava*, the finest champagne in Europe outside of France, and a lot cheaper.

One writer has noted that in Cataluña "fish is practically a religion, shellfish practically a cult." You worshiped faithfully by eating saw-toothed monkfish, a creature as tasty as it is ugly; thick steaks of bream and tuna, silky red mullet, silvery fresh sardines roasted over a wooden fire, baby eels cooked in olive oil and sliced red peppers, scallops with meat as opalescent as Botticelli's Venus, fat shrimp barely poached in sea salt, reddish-brown baby octopus, tangled squid and cuttlefish, goose barnacles, mussels, spiny lobsters with flesh as sweet as fresh butter; *suquet de peix*, the Catalan bouillabaisse simmered from the day's catch with garlic, tomatoes, almonds, saffron, parsley and anything the chef might toss in. Some dishes had such bracing freshness, flavors so penetrating that they seemed to fill one's veins with seawater.

You took the train south to Barcelona. There you hoped to explore the city and bring in the New Year. After spending time on the coast, the metropolis seemed dull and grey in contrast, like Los Angeles after a drive from Big Sur. Even Antoni Gaudí's designs, with their wavy balconies, twisting walls and fairy-tale towers, looked ghostly in the damp air. His towering *Sagrada Familia*, the Expiatory

Temple of the Holy Family, perhaps the world's most famous unfinished building, resembled the roofless, naked shell of a church bombed in an air raid, a sort of drip-castle Coventry Cathedral in Cataluña, unredeemed by a heroic past. It might have stood for the mood of postwar Spain: a Gothic structure seemingly in ruins, "*en obras*" or under repair beneath a skeleton of scaffolds, whose architect had been killed by a streetcar, an appropriate emblem of modernity.

The open-air and covered markets of Barcelona relieved the impression of a drab, dying city. There men and women shopped for food, whiffed and touched it, questioned, haggled, bargained, bought and sold as peoples have done for thousands of years in this vast emporium, the Mediterranean Basin. At La Boqueria, the cavernous central market, workers carried boxes, bags, cages with rabbits and squawking chickens inside, farmers pulled bleating lambs and goats on halters, while hunters bore racks of soft-feathered game birds hung with beak down, dripping blood. The stalls of pink-faced butchers displayed bleeding quarters of beef, veal, lamb, pork—whole pigs, parts of pigs, closed-eyed cochinillos, suckling pigs; braids of salame, chorizo, morcilla, light and dark Catalan *butifarra*, deep-red jamón serrano. You saw marble tables with iced baskets and trays of seafood: all the fishes you had eaten on the Costa Brava and more, dried salt cod, smoky tuna fillets or *mojama* from Murcia, precious salted roe or *hueva*, a Spanish version of caviar.

You visited stalls with wooden crates of fruits and vegetables, hundreds of herbs and spices, freshly picked or dried, including delicate, reddish-yellow stems of saffron, valuable as a bride's dowry; legumes in more colors than a rainbow; earthy mushrooms, brown, grey, white, orange and yellow—cepes, morels, chanterelles and others whose names have no translation; black truffles smelling of the forest floor, almost worth their weight in gold, live snails with soil stuck to their mottled shells, twisted loops of garlic, barrels of anchovies in brine, jars of marinated olives, wheels of young or aged local cheeses like Mató, Urgellet, La Garrotxa, Montsec, Serrat; dried, roasted or candied fruits and nuts; pastries, tarts, cakes, cookies, fritters.

You decided to buy some fruit to take back to your pensión in downtown Barcelona. An old woman who sold the best apples could barely speak Castilian. She must have been from a small village where Catalan was the first language. Seeing the problem, a young couple with a child came to your rescue, serving as interpreters and dickering for a better price to boot. Afterwards you invited them for a drink at one of the cafés near the market.

Jordi and Núria were both lawyers who worked in labor rights, a heroic field in fascist Spain, where the state set wages, outlawed unions and quashed strikes. Their son Jordi Jr., whom they called by his nickname of Toti, was a handsome boy of three with a head as large and proud as a Roman bust. He was also one of the best-behaved children you had seen anywhere, sitting like a small adult in his own chair, smiling at us and the passers-by, drinking hot chocolate without spilling more than a few drops, calling you "*el señor americano.*" The four of us talked for almost two hours until Toti got restless, showing that he was just a child after all. We had struck a friendship so quickly that it seemed we had known each other for months.

On New Year's Eve they invited you and several neighbors to their apartment on Las Ramblas, the long, tree-lined avenue that divides the old town in two. Until that night you had never crossed the threshold of a private home in the Peninsula. Like most southern Europeans, the Spaniards—and Catalans, many of whom did not consider themselves Spanish—preferred to meet in public places, rarely opening their cramped dwellings to social life. Unlike Americans they did not leave their children behind with babysitters or family, bringing them along for the party.

In Jordi's and Núria's house we listened to records by Raimon, Salomé and other valiant young singers who were defying the regime by performing some of their songs in Catalan. As we drank one bottle of cava after another, our host and the other men made their toast of *"Salut e força al canut!"* To your health and may your pecker stay proud! At midnight all of us, including the children, crowded onto a small balcony to eat the customary twelve grapes to the ringing of church bells throughout the city, making a wish between each stroke to bring luck for the new year. How could you have divined what fortune would be yours in 1965?

Your hosts persuaded you to remain in Barcelona until Epiphany, the Twelfth Night of Christmas, Eve of the Magi, the Three Wise Men who bring presents to boys and girls like Santa Claus in northern Europe and the U.S. By now your funds were getting low, but Jordi and Núria were buying and serving so many meals that you could postpone the return to Madrid. Their families congregated at a country house in San Cugat del Vallès, twenty miles north of Barcelona, to celebrate the end of the two-week holiday: great-grandparents, grandparents, parents, sons and daughters, brothers and sisters, cousins, great-grandchildren and grandchildren, aunts and uncles, nieces and nephews.

After we drank cava and ate a plentiful lunch, the boys and girls performed the regional tradition of pounding a yule log with a club as they chanted:

¡Caga tiet,
Caga turrons de Nadal,
Caga pardal!

Shit, uncle,
Shit Christmas candies,
Shit a whole bunch of them!

Normally they perform the ritual on Christmas Eve, but little Toti had insisted that it be repeated for "el señor americano." As you watched him and his cousins smack the wood and sing those verses, you tried to picture, without success, American kids ordering Santa Claus to shit candy canes under a Christmas tree.

Then it was your turn to wield the staff, hefty as a billy club. You whacked the yule log as though it were a *piñata,* and wood chips flew around the room while Jordi shouted *"Collons de Déu!"* By the balls of God!—an expression you don't remember hearing at home either. Everyone showered you with bars of *turrón,* the nougat made of honey, eggs and almonds, coated with diaphanous wafer, a specialty since the Arabs occupied this land. We ended by drinking more cava and eating *tortell de Reis,* cake of the Kings, stuffed with marzipan, decorated with glazed oranges, limes and cherries. One of the children found a lucky charm in the white dough: a figurine of the Magi. For the first time you knew the joy of being surrounded by the warmth of a family in this Old World.

That night the Three Kings would bring you a greater gift from the East.

9. Khedidja

In a pool of light from a street lamp, where the acacias had been strung with banners for Epiphany, you saw her. She made you feel so dizzy that you might have been standing on the highest tower of the Sagrada Familia.

If she had not been walking on the Ramblas, alone, at three o'clock in the morning, nobody would have known why she was there. Khedidja did not need to wear thick makeup, gaudy colors, a mini-skirt or spiked heels. It was enough to see her under the light— her slim ankles, blue-black hair and magnolia skin—to realize your life had been wasted until that moment. She spoke little Spanish, no English. She barely understood pesetas. Talking as much with her hands as with her lips, she told you her name. She tried to convey that she had arrived recently in Barcelona. From where? From across the sea, Khedidja managed to impart with gestures and mysterious words. Her throaty accent sounded like a patois of French and another language—maybe Arabic, you guessed from her name.

You led her to the square in front of your pensión. Trying to impress Khedidja with your savoir faire, you clapped so hard for the sereno that your hands stung in the night air. Then you shouted in a stentorian voice, imitating the Spaniards you had heard so often— "Se—reée—no!"—hoping, wishing, praying he would arrive fast. You felt the urgency of desire, jealous of every man who slowed to look unbelievingly at Khedidja, lustrous at your side beneath a street light. By the time the watchman appeared, a pack of idolaters was pacing around us, men with hands in their pockets against the cold, staring in common wonder.

The sereno approached, grumbling while he searched through his keys. The instant he spotted Khedidja, his demeanor brightened: he grinned, stood straight as a rod and made friendly chatter while he opened the door. Knowing this night would cost dearly, you gave him just a few pieces of loose change. As Khedidja entered, the watchman winked at you and twirled an invisible mustache with the thumb and forefinger of his right hand—some Mediterranean gesture of male complicity, you surmised. *"Que tengan ustedes muy buenas noches,"* he told us, May both of you have a very good night.

We climbed the creaking stairs to the third floor. We stepped into the room, Khedidja removed your jacket, slipped out of her coat and hung them together on a hook behind the door. Talking under her breath, singing to herself in her puzzling language, she gamboled about the place as though she were inspecting a new apartment, turning on the only lamp, drawing the curtains here, dusting off the lone table, smoothing the bed and pillows there, running hot and cold water in the tiny bathroom. In a few minutes she had effaced the walls stained by moisture, transformed the feeble light bulb, the unglazed sink, the plastic bidet, the bedspread marked by past nights of nausea or love.

After putting the site in order, Khedidja took your wrist gently and walked you to the room's sole chair. She sat on the armrest next to you, sighing, satisfied for completing her task. She crossed her legs encased in black stockings. Seeing Khedidja close now, you perceived how young she must be—not more than twenty-two or so, your own age. You looked deeply into her eyes, their night-black pupils with black rings around their yellow-green irises. A minute later we were both squeezed into the chair, no longer feeling the cold, making an effort to converse in macaronic Spanish, French or Italian, having more luck with shrugs, grimaces, smiles and touches.

Without warning she rose to her feet. Khedidja turned off the lamp, leaving us in semi-darkness. The curtains filtered light from the street. On the far side of the room she began to undress, humming the tune she had sung before. With a flick of each ankle she let her high-heeled shoes fall to the wooden floor. As Khedidja disrobed, you could hear the chiming of her necklaces and bracelets against muffled noises from the square below. Once her garments lay in a small pile at her feet, she turned her torso at a three-quarter angle, swaying like a palm tree on a dune. Her silhouette stood out in the shadows: upturned breasts, wasp-like waist, spreading hips. As your eyes grew accustomed to the half-light, you discerned a line of down from her navel to the shadow of her loins, her calves tapering to thin ankles. (How could you fail to recall Concepción's words about the most passionate women?) On one of her legs you noticed a golden anklet, then the glint of a ring on a toe of her foot.

Murmuring her guttural tones, Khedidja came to the chair again, where she helped you stand. Slowly, whispering unfamiliar words, she took off your shirt and undershirt, folding them carefully, placing them on the seat before she knelt and unlaced your shoes. As she had done, you shook each ankle in turn, nearly losing your balance before your shoes struck the floor. She smiled in recognition. While she rose to her feet, unclasped your belt and lowered your pants and underwear, you breathed in the fragrance of Khedidja's body, holding it in your nostrils, feeling it rise to your head, mingle there with the cava.

She led you to the bathroom, no larger than a closet, where she sat you on the bidet. With soap and lukewarm water Khedidja washed you from the waist down, converting the yellow plastic basin into a fount of resplendent porcelain with foaming waters. After drying you with a red towel, she straddled the bidet, making it clear that you should administer the same ablutions. You wet her thighs, her soft center, silky and warmer than the tepid water, burning your palm as you held it there. *"Le savon,"* Khedidja requested with a peal of laughter. Those two words seemed to waken you, as though you had forgotten the soap, the water, everything but her.

You washed and rinsed Khedidja, trying to pat her dry as she squirmed, giggled and dismounted the bidet. Playing tug-o'-war with the towel, we stumbled toward the bed, tore off the covers, fell down together, bouncing on squeaky springs. There the red towel became a booty of war, a scourge, belt, girdle, sash, loincloth, skirt, robe, mask, turban, even a towel while we soaked the sheets in the water from the bidet and the heat of our bodies. Stars whirled in the night and Khedidja's name scalds your memory.

You see her curled on the sheets the next morning, dowered in her jewelry—rings, bracelets, necklaces, earrings, anklet, toe ring. Later she would allow you to love her without those appendages, save for the last two. Those she wore always. Her anklet and toe ring had been crafted by a goldsmith in the old Medina quarter of Tunis, her hometown, she would tell you, who had fitted them snugly, leaving so little play in each that they could only be removed by cutting through the metal. It was just as well. Khedidja had assimilated those two pieces so utterly to herself that they were parts of her small white extremity, employed at whimsical moments in the most unimaginable ways. On her anklet and toe ring the artisan had imprinted his seal: a pair of minute crescent moons. You cannot recall them without a shudder, those ornaments molded to the contour of her left ankle, of her first toe on the same foot.

A pounding on the door expelled you from the paradise of contemplating Khedidja in her sleep. You roused yourself, staggered from the bed, cracked the door and saw the owner of the pensión in the hallway. The man craned his neck to peer into the room, claiming that we had kept him awake last night, that some of his permanent residents had complained. Without asking permission, he stuck his head through the door, sniffing the air. In your half-sleep his face distorted itself into an elephantine, wriggling nose seen through a fisheye lens.

"This is a respectable house!" the owner screamed in Spanish with the harsh accent of Barcelona. "We don't permit *fulanas* on our premises! *Qué desmadre!* What a scandal! I'm going to call the police if you're not out of here by ten o'clock this morning!" The man shut the door in your face.

The rest was trying to stir Khedidja from her primordial sleep, awaken her without being drawn again into her warm, humid Eden. She moaned, turned, cooed, then sprung at you with the reeking towel in one hand, wrestled and pulled you onto the sheets. You wrapped it around her waist, attempting to lift her from the bed while the force of desire or gravity towed you down dreamily, floatingly down to Khedidja.

Between trips to the bidet and the bathroom we succeeded in packing your suitcase, vacating our room, dashing downstairs as the church bells were tolling ten o'clock. When we reached the plaza below, we turned to look up at our window on the third floor. A triumphant, red banner of love was hanging from the balcony, waving in the breeze.

Surrounded by dozens of flower shops and cages with birds for sale, we had breakfast at an outdoor café on the Ramblas. Pedestrians walked along the avenue, the trams were running, the city had gone back to work after the holy days. When you grazed Khedidja's arm, she glanced up with lakelike eyes. You pointed at the suitcase, then the street, inclining your head on a make-believe pillow.

She captured your meaning. *"Ah, chercher nouvelle pension,"* she stated, with some inscrutable words thrown in. Khedidja pouted her lips. *"*You stay my *appartement* few days." Hardly believing your ears, silently you thanked the Black Virgin, the shitting uncle, the Wise Men—the whole pantheon of gods, semi-gods and goddesses of Cataluña and the world for their munificence.

You looked up at the first cloudless sky you had seen in Barcelona. Flowers overflowed the stalls around us, sparrows darted in and out of trees, caged parrots sang in a morning riot. You understood why a poet called these Ramblas the happiest street in the world, why he wanted it to go on forever.

Khedidja had moved into a humble neighborhood near the port that week, not far from the spot where we met on the glowing madrugada of January 6, 1965. Although she had been there only three days, the apartment had received her imprint: a Tunisian rug in the center of the small living room, two or three silk wall hangings with Arabesque designs, little brass incense burners in the corners. The floors, walls, counters, furniture—everything appeared immaculate. Just as a middle-class woman might yearn for Khedidja's freedom, you would figure out later, she must have aspired to bourgeois stability. After all she had not been named for one of Mohammed's concubines but for the wealthy widow who became his wife, his faithful convert and disciple.

Needless to say, you did not rush to find new lodgings. You placed a long-distance call to your apartment building in Madrid, where old José's widow answered in the doorman's booth. Could she kindly instruct the landlord to cancel the lease, for which you would of course surrender the deposit; could she also empty your sparse belongings and keep them for herself? When the good woman assented, you added her to the roll of benefactors, the guardian spirits, the host of seraphim who were joining forces to keep you with Khedidja.

You also phoned the director of the language school, notifying him that you would not return to Madrid for the time being. Finally you called Rodrigo, who guessed the reason for your absence. "*Cuidado, Eduardo,*" he warned. "*El amor y el vino sacan al hombre de tino,*" Love and wine turn a man's mind.

While you perfunctorily sought a new pensión, Khedidja helped you discover a Barcelona that neither of us could have found alone. For the first time you knew the joy of exploring a new metropolis with a woman. You feared that we might cross Jordi and Núria on the streets—to whom you had already pronounced farewell—or their family and friends, but the anonymity of the great city veiled us beneath its sheltering wings.

We walked up and down tree-lined avenues, passing people and more people, on cobbled alleys in the Barrio Gótico, streets and more streets, parks, plazas, gardens, patios. Whenever we came to a fountain, Khedidja paused to look, to wet her hands and face, to splash you. She had the Arabs' devotion to running water, the same that drove the Moors to fill their palaces with pools, cascades, wells and cisterns in Al-Andalus, their dominion that stretched from the Pyrenees to Gibraltar, encompassing the very city where we were living. Khedidja enjoyed breaking the taboos of her religion, drinking wine and eating ham, sausage and shellfish. For us every table was a feast. We favored La Barceloneta, the fishermen's and workmen's quarter, where eateries stood on stilts along a strip of dirty beach. In those breezy dining rooms, looking out to sea, Khedidja would order her favorite dish, Catalan pasta or *fideuà*, simmered in a dark fish stock and served with a dab of garlicky *allioli*. Nobody could have made eating look more sensuous, slurping her noodles from an earthenware dish.

From the port we would stroll along the Paseo de Colón to the bronze statue of Christopher Columbus that sits atop a soaring iron column. The explorer is not pointing west toward the Atlantic and the New World, as one might expect, but southeast toward the Mediterranean and Tunisia. Everything conspired to prefigure your life with Khedidja in a dizzying tower of pleasure.

By this hour the streets had emptied, stores were closed, and most of Barcelona appeared to be asleep. The siesta was a hallowed custom that the monarchy, the Republic or Franco could not have changed. (Why would they have wanted to? It creates contented citizens.) Only in Spain would opposing armies defer combat for the midday rest, a practice observed by both sides in the Civil War. We also suspended engagements for a long nap. How you recall those siestas after lunch on cool winter afternoons! Sometimes Khedidja would awake with a curly lock of black hair across her forehead, pushing it away in her half-sleep, it falling back on her brow like the foretoken of a wrinkle or age.

When we walked up the Ramblas afterwards, an absurd kind of joy would clasp us by the waist. Even the most dreary alley abounded in surprises. Khedidja started singing or making jokes you could barely understand but which seemed hilarious at the moment—about a lopsided parrot in a cage, a salesman who leered as we walked by, birds that darted in and out of trees, leaving their droppings on kiosks or pedestrians. (They never hit us, who were shielded by a company of angels.) She was showing you how to look and see where you thought there was nothing, just her way of stopping suddenly to watch a cloud slip behind a rooftop, to admire an elegant man dressed in a tailored suit, to duck into a patio with a spurting fountain, potted ferns and geraniums where an old woman was knitting socks. Then there were the animals, the mangy mutts disarmed by her petting—Khedidja did not share the Muslim aversion to dogs—or emaciated cats rubbing against her legs as she communed with them by words, strokes, whispers.

One day we saw a gypsy woman nursing a brown baby in the folds of her bosom. (You remembered Alfa and her son in Tijuana.) On her back she carried a load of paper flowers, each as big and round as a frisbee—bright oranges, pinks, yellows—flaring suns, fireworks, a ferris wheel of flowers. Khedidja bought them all, somehow informing the woman that we would take them to our apartment, the gypsy refusing to let us carry them by ourselves, the three (four) of us wedging through crowds as the two ladies from the East spoke their female language of eyes hands smiles until we arrived at the building, where we said goodbye, *"Dios les bendiga,"* the mother repeated with the baby at her breast. We balanced our purchase between the two of us, passing the concierge who glared from her dim cubicle, then climbing the stairs, almost losing the full bouquet when we opened the door and rushed in, dropping our prize, crushing the galaxy of paper flowers as we rolled on the floor, kissed, hugged and mounted Khedidja's magic carpet. *"Quiero amor, mi vida,"* she said in her strange accent, trying the new words she had learned in Spanish.

Our second paradise lasted longer than our first at the pensión. You recall everything about her. Khedidja tiptoeing barefoot through the shallow water on a beach at Cadaqués, rapturous but with the Bedouin suspicion of the sea. Khedidja wanting to buy an original drawing at the Picasso Museum in the Gothic Quarter—two pairs of red lips seeking each other, close but never touching—failing to comprehend it was not for sale, that it was priceless. Khedidja burning incense as soon as we entered her apartment, to purify the air, cleanse the dirt of the city from our lungs with cedar, sandalwood and musk. (The Three Kings had carried incense too.) Khedidja preparing our coffee black as night, the two of us drinking it together in demitasses heaped with sugar. Khedidja reading the grinds at the bottom of your cup, foretelling many sons but little wealth, great joy in love combined with great sadness. (Did she know that she was wealth and joy enough?) Khedidja eating an orange, smiling as the juice dripped from the corners of her mouth, her pointed tongue darting between her teeth to lick the acid sweetness. Khedidja playing records by Om Kalthoum ("I still remember"), by Faiza Ahmed ("When will you come to me?") and other singers whose names you never understood, humming to the music as we embraced on the parquet floor and rode her flying rug before gliding, drifting back to earth. Khedidja asleep in the powdery light of morning, the down beneath her arms, the path of fuzz sloping from her belly to her darkest root.

Listening to a song of tragic love by Om Kalthoum one night, she spread your map of the Mediterranean on the floor. We had just returned from the beach and dinner at Sitges. The warmth of the sun lingered on our bodies, grains of sand in our ears and shoes. Khedidja pointed to the place in Tunisia (Afrikiya, she called it) where her family lived, near the site of ancient Carthage. You showed her the town where your grandfather had been born in the province of Palermo. With amazement we saw that Tunisia and Sicily were less than a hundred miles apart. Both had been invaded, colonized, settled more or less by Phoenicians, Carthaginians, Romans, Jews, Vandals, Arabs, Spaniards, French—largely the peoples and tribes who had written the story of Spain too. Khedidja's ancestors, the Arabs, had lived in the Iberian Peninsula longer than Europeans had occupied the New World; the Jews had been there even longer.

Although she was legally a foreigner, she was a Spaniard in a way that you could never be: Khedidja was proto-Spanish. Northern Africa, Spain, Sicily, they belonged to the archaic Mediterranean rim, cradle of cultures. Living with Khedidja during those radiant weeks in Barcelona, you were nearly coming home to that domain, to your own blood and history.

Before you could find a cheap pensión or apartment in the neighborhood, your savings had been depleted. When you started to broach the subject with Khedidja, she would catch you in the silken web that she spun around us, smothering your words. Anyway you had learned that loving such a woman filled every hour, leaving no time or will to work.

One afternoon while we were drinking coffee—it had never tasted so bitter—you summoned courage to confess the truth. Khedidja did not look shocked or dismayed, as though she had anticipated this news.

"Moi regrette," she told you. "Devoir aider—'um, al'akhawat, al'iikhwa", she tried to explain, reverting to Arabic when she spoke of her family. She rubbed her first two fingers and her thumb together in the universal sign for money, a gesture that seemed too crass for such a white, delicate hand. Frowning and biting her lip, she hesitated as though she had more to say. But Khedidja remained silent. When her eyes appeared to mist, she concealed them beneath her dark lashes, lowering her head. "Désolée, habib."

"I'm sorry too—so sorry, Khedidja." She did not look up. Suspecting she might not feel what you felt for her, that she might have lived through all of this before, you said nothing else. Did she also know it would hurt less to end it now?

If you lost your virginity in Mexico, you lost your innocence in Spain. More a gain than a loss: Khedidja taught you that the human body is inexhaustible, that the way to the soul may pass through the tender, mortal flesh. Such elation could not have endured. You had taken her away from work, now you would pay the price: she had to support her mother, sisters, brothers. As long as you could share some of her expenses, she had stayed with you, perhaps because you knew Spanish and made her first weeks in Barcelona easier, less lonely.

Before an exterminating angel could drive you from her Eden, you packed your suitcase one morning at dawn. For the last time you watched her as she slept. "Hasta siempre," you whispered and turned, pulling against a riptide. You walked down the stairs to the empty street, where you fell to your knees and sobbed.

Today you imagine Khedidja living in Marseilles, Genoa, Palermo, Algiers, Tunis or some other antique metropolis on the coast. Through a window she stares at the sea, our sea, *Mare Nostrum,* our Mediterranean. She must have known great sadness and joy in love.

10. Valencia

You took a boat from Barcelona to Palma de Mallorca, thinking the water and distance would help dissolve the memories. But the Mediterranean, that lake of love, evoked Khedidja even more. On an island with white beaches, a sinuous coast and secluded *calas*, transparent, peacock-blue coves, how could you fail to recall her and her fascination with water and the sea?

It was easy finding work in Palma, where the locals needed English to attend the growing number of foreigners. In the morning you taught classes downtown. During the long Spanish lunch you traveled to the beaches, returning for a second round of lessons in the early evening. The weather had warmed enough for swimming, if not for the natives at least for you and the occasional *sueca* or "Swedish girl"—the Spaniards' term for a female visitor from northern Europe, whatever her nationality. If the travel writer Richard Ford were alive, you thought, he might have to alter his depiction of Spain to "Bullfights, bandits, blue and black eyes."

Floating on your back in the soft current, you thought that a new sea, this Mediterranean, and a new ocean, the Atlantic, had almost been too much in three months. You watched the mutation of clouds in the Mallorcan sky: caravans in a pure white desert, turbaned heads of prophets, palm trees on undulating dunes. In the late Spanish night you listened to jazz at Las Cuevas del Molino, a club on the coast, remembering.

By the middle of March you had saved enough to travel again. You boarded a boat from Palma to Valencia, several hundred miles south of Barcelona on the coast, where you had arranged to meet an old friend. Since hotels and pensiones were full for the local celebration of the *Fallas*, you rented a room in a private apartment.

Doña Claudia stood about 4'10" and must have been at least sixty years old. From the start she made it clear that her home was not a boardinghouse. *"Mi casa es muy respetable,"* she announced or warned. (You recalled the owner of the pensión in Barcelona.) Once a year she rented out a bedroom for the explosive festival that culminates on the feast of St. Joseph, the first day of spring.

"I do this not for money," Doña Claudia insisted, "but for my civic duty. So outsiders like you can live with a family and enjoy the customs of Valencia." Since the woman appeared to live alone, you wondered what she meant by "family."

"Gracias, Señora. My friend will enjoy your hospitality and the customs too. He arrives this evening."

"Is he also American?"

"Sí, Señora."

"Good. I rent exclusively to foreigners."

"Do you mind if I ask why?"

"Bueno," she answered, which could mean anything, good or bad. "Because they always pay on time. And I know they will leave after the *feria*." Doña Claudia cupped her hands and confided, *"Sabe usted una cosa?* Do you know something? One cannot get rid of Spaniards—you rent to them for a week and they want to stay forever." The woman said these words as if her compatriots belonged to a separate country. You smiled, remembering Doña Hortensia, your landlady in Mexico. She and Doña Claudia would get along fine.

Valencia on the eve of the fiesta had an air of seething expectation. The station teemed with travelers, their families and friends. Rich stepped off the train: 6'2" with a manifestly American face, build and clothes—white T-shirt, blue jeans, tennis shoes. He had promised to bring your portable typewriter from home, but he was not carrying a suitcase or handbag. As we walked toward our room in the cool Valencian night, surrounded by other pedestrians, he told you his story.

"You won't believe this, man. On the train from Paris to Madrid I met a Spaniard who spoke a little English. He told me that he knew a cheap pensión where we could share a room and save money." Rich stopped, pointing to three enormous platforms at a crossroads, all surmounted by colorful, larger-than-life figures. "What in the hell are those things?"

"Those are fallas, one of the reasons we're in Valencia."

"They sort of remind me of the Rose Parade."

"I guess they're built like the floats in Pasadena. But they're covered with papier-mâché instead of flowers and their subjects are entirely different. You'll see."

"Anyhow this guy named Paco took me to the pensión in Madrid," Rich said as we continued walking on the crowded street. "The place was a dive but cheap as dirt—we shared a double room for a couple of dollars each." In his mind your friend still converted prices into a familiar currency, while you already figured and counted in pesetas.

"So what happened?"

"Paco showed me around Madrid. I felt so unsure of myself that it was easy to rely on him—remember this is my first trip abroad and I hardly know any Spanish."

"Go on."

"On the second night he asked me if I wanted to see a film at a theater near the pensión, a kind of soft-porn flick."

"That's the only kind of porn in Spain."

"After we started watching the movie, Paco said he was going to the bathroom. He didn't return for about ten minutes so I decided to get up and look for him." Rich paused to observe another falla at an intersection. "I searched everywhere," he went on, "in the lobby, the bathrooms, the entrance. Then I got this feeling in my gut that something was wrong, really wrong." He shivered, whether from the recollection or the night air. "I ran back to the pension, raced up the stairs, unlocked the door and saw the room turned upside down." Rich's voice grew louder. "The son of a bitch had cleaned it out—his stuff, mine, the money I had hidden in a drawer, my suitcase, everything, your typewriter too. All I had left were the clothes on my back—what I'm wearing now—my passport and my wallet."

"*Menos mal,*" you murmured to yourself, At least there's that. By this time you had begun to think, even to dream in Spanish.

You had never seen your friend look so dejected. How could you cheer him? "Rich, do you know what they do here at a moment like this?"

"How could I? I just arrived in the fucking country four days ago."

"Don't call it that—it's my country too."

"What do you mean, man?"

"I had a great-great-grandmother from Spain."

"No kidding. So tell me what Spaniards do at a moment like this."

"Have a drink, of course."

We stepped into a bar: in Spain one is always there when you need it. The space was full of men of all ages, smoking, drinking, talking, laughing, shouting. In those days Spanish fiestas remained a masculine prerogative. For women they only meant more work behind the scenes, cooking, washing and cleaning.

You pushed toward the bar and called for two *claras con limón,* lagers infused with lemon soda. With the squeamish attitude of most Americans, Rich stood behind the crush of drinkers, looking out of place. You understood how he might be tempted to rely on someone like Paco, as you had depended on Zanahorio.

"To better luck," you toasted as we clinked our pint glasses.

"This stuff is good—more thirst-quenching than straight beer."

"Right. You know Rich, I miss my old Olivetti."

"I'm sorry about the typewriter. For me the worst part wasn't the theft, the stolen things, even the money. It was knowing I'd trusted somebody who betrayed me, and now I was alone in a foreign country." A vulnerable smile crossed Rich's face. "At least I could look forward to meeting you, Ed. You sure know your way around here."

It sounded odd to hear your American name. For the past four months everyone had addressed you as Eduardo. (Except for her, who called you Édouard and *chéri* in French, habib and untranslatable words in Arabic.)

To grasp the situation you would have to know more about Rich. You would have to learn that he was handsome and muscular, that he had been the starting pitcher and the captain of our high school baseball team, the boyfriend of the loveliest girl on campus. Every other male in the student body viewed him with green-eyed envy. You would have to know that this incarnation of youthful American prowess, Richie Arnault, was now confessing that he relied on me—a benchwarmer in sports, a writer for the school newspaper who reported his one-hitters, no-hitters, strikeouts, shutouts and victories in the playoffs. Then you would understand how it felt to be the one in charge, drinking a sweat-beaded beer with him on the eve of Fallas.

You told Rich something you had barely thought before. "I like this country so much that I might decide to live here someday."

"Not me. What's so good about it?"

"Wait and see."

Rich looked for a spot to set his glass. He could not find a square inch of free space on the bar, the tables or anywhere. "Will you hold my drink while I blow my nose, Ed?"

"Sure." Pointing at his T-shirt, you said, "You'll need something warmer at night."

"You know why I have this cold, don't you? Ever since that bastard robbed my clothes, I don't have anything else to wear. It pisses me off that he got the black leather jacket my girlfriend gave me for Christmas."

For a second you recalled Kathy, whose waves of blond hair had enthralled us in school. You asked, "Do you think Paco had the whole thing planned from the start, from the time he met you on the train?"

"I wouldn't put it past him—the fucker was smooth as oil. He told me that he'd been to the fairs in Seville and Pamplona. I think he travels the country from place to place, working the fiestas the way a gambler works the tracks, hunting for dumb-ass victims like me."

When we finished our drinks, you paid the total that the bartender had scribbled on the counter in white chalk.

"Why don't we go Dutch?" Rich asked.

"Because it's your first night in Valencia and I want to buy your drink. Also because it's the custom here—one person pays. Next time will be your turn."

Rich paused before replying. "If you say," he said, frowning.

"Sometimes you get stuck with a bigger tab," you tried to reassure him, "sometimes a smaller one—it's luck of the draw. But in the end it works out. The Spanish style is a lot more elegant without all the dickering."

As we left the bar, Rich said nothing. He was going to have trouble adjusting to this country. In contrast you already embraced the Spanish practice of generosity and other usages as the normal manner of doing things. You regarded the groups of men around us on the streets and sidewalks, all of them animated, geared up for the Fallas, the most important week of their year. In a sense I'm closer to them, you thought, those nameless Valencians, than to Rich, a Californian like me, a friend since high school. You were in the early stages of becoming a sort of naturalized visitor in Spain, a denaturalized resident of America. You probably did not think like this at the time, but you felt it on your skin, in your head, walking through the streets of a Spanish city for the first time with an American.

We reached another platform in the middle of a palm-lined square. Moving closer, we saw what we could not believe: the tableau depicted John Kennedy's assassination, an occurrence more tragic and distant than the mostly playful scenes on other floats. The figure of Lee Harvey Oswald appeared as a Pinocchio-like marionette over the fallen president, its strings manipulated by a crew of misshapen gangsters with gargoyle faces. The gaudy, oversized images, illuminated by street lights in the plaza, made the stage look grotesque, a hallucination of the historical images we knew too well.

Staring up at the tableau, Rich said, "This place is different, Ed."

"That's what I like about it."

When we reached the apartment, Doña Claudia greeted us. You introduced Rich. She scrutinized him to determine if he was worthy of her reputable home. Since he knew little Spanish, she turned to you. "Should I call him Ricardo?"

"Sí, Señora."

Rich understood. "Like Ricardo Montalbán," he mumbled in your ear.

"Does he not have luggage?" she asked.

"He travels lightly, Señora."

"Tell your friend he's going to catch his death of cold without a jacket."

"I told him that."

"He should know better," she said with a sigh. "I've already turned back the sheets of your beds, hijos. Tomorrow morning I'll serve breakfast between ten and ten thirty." Rich must have picked up a few of Doña Claudia's words, because he shot you a smile, no doubt amused by this peculiar woman and her tardy Spanish schedule. "Buenas noches, *jóvenes*," she bid us. She turned and shuffled to her room.

In the morning we went to the kitchen one at a time in order to make it easier for our hostess. When Rich returned to our room, he asked, "Why does she keep talking about constipation? She must have mentioned it five times. Does she do the same with you?"

"Nope."

We spent that day and others in the street, eating and drinking, viewing floats, parades of boys, girls, men and women in their traditional costumes, displays of fireworks; listening to brass bands or *dolçainas* and *tabalets*, local wind and percussion instruments; eating and drinking more. We covered miles of the city, exploring one zone after another—the old Arab, medieval and Renaissance quarter downtown, newer neighborhoods farther out, desolate barrios near the river. With the exception of its historic enclave Valencia had become an ugly city, marred by uncontrolled development during the postwar years. It did not matter. The character of this and other Spanish towns lies largely in people, not in architecture or city planning.

At 5:30 sharp each afternoon we were seated in the *plaza de toros:* bullfights were the most punctual events in Spain. Together we watched the death of animals raised by renowned breeders like Carlos Núñez, Conde de la Corte, Álvaro Domecq, Fermín Bohórquez. We saw toreros like young Francisco Rivera "Paquirri," Julio Aparicio, unsmiling Miguel Báez "Litri," Jaime Ostos, otherworldly Santiago Martín "El Viti," who showed the Castilian zeal for death as he plunged over the animal's withers for the *estocada* or kill. After seeing so many corridas here and in Mexico, you no longer felt fastidious about the ordained sacrifice.

To his credit your friend learned quickly. When a couple of British tourists committed the common gaffe of "rooting" for the bulls, failing to understand that toreo is not a sporting match but a tragic spectacle, Rich asked, "Why don't the Spaniards kick them out?"

"They're too polite. Those Brits believe the corrida's barbaric but they're the only barbarians in the crowd."

"You know what I like about the bullfights?"

"What?"

"The way everything, every move has a right and a wrong way of doing it."

"Your catching on, Rich. You could say the same thing about the whole country."

Afterwards we moved with the crowds into bars and cafés, where we drank, ate tapas, drank more, returning to the apartment before dawn. After the *Nit del Foc* or Night of Fire on the eve of San José, when some three thousand kilos of fireworks were detonated over the dry bed of the River Turia at 1:30 in the morning, Rich had been won over. He had caught the spirit despite his unshakable cold, turning into a good partner for the Fallas. By that time the tension of the feria had mounted, it all began to seem unreal, and we sensed that unpredictable things would happen.

Each day after breakfast Rich had returned to the room with the same story about our landlady's obsession. We had decided to satisfy our curiosity, advising Doña Claudia that the two of us would eat together on the last morning, March 19th, climax of the fair.

The day dawned sunless, the light clouded like a pearl. Doña Claudia bemoaned the weather as she prepared our breakfast, worrying that rain would spoil the final revels for us, dampen the momentous burning of floats. She had bought fresh-baked Mallorcan *ensaimadas* for the occasion—rich, soft, flaky, spiraled rolls sprinkled with powdered sugar—to compliment the usual café con leche and juice squeezed from luscious Valencian oranges. The widow even invited us to sit in her dining room instead of the kitchen.

Doña Claudia served on a carved mahogany table. "Do you mind if I join you this morning?" she asked with a smile.

"*Claro que no,*" you answered. She must have been apprehensive about her solitude after the Fallas.

"Gracias, hijos," she told us. Doña Claudia took a chair at the table's head. "This is where my husband used to sit. I lost him seven years ago."

"*Lo sentimos mucho,* Señora."

Tears seeped from our landlady's brown eyes. "With the two of you here it feels like a family."

Rich asked in broken Spanish, "Did you have children, Doña Claudia?"

She looked away. "No."

What could we say to fill the silence that followed the woman's words? Then you recalled the phrase in Spanish for a lull in conversation. "*Ha pasado un ángel,*" An angel must have passed by, you told her.

"*Debe ser,*" Must be that, she whispered sadly, averting her eyes again. Doña Claudia recovered enough to ask, "Do you and Ricardo like our Valencian food?"

"*Naturalmente,* Señora," you responded for both of us.

"Sí, Señora," Rich added.

"Have you eaten paella?"

"Not here but I had it several times in Madrid." You turned to Rich, who was following the conversation better than I thought.

"No, Señora."

"Then it wasn't paella, jóvenes. There is just one place in the world where you can eat the real thing—here, in Valencia." At that instant your friend sneezed. "*Sigues constipado, Ricardo?*" the woman inquired. You grasped it: the word *constipado* simply means "congested" in Spain.

Without answering our landlady's question, Rich looked at you with a shit-eating grin. "See what I mean?" he said between his teeth.

You did not bother to explain. You were enjoying the misunderstanding at both his and the widow's expense. Being the only one who spoke fluent Spanish and English, you could have played off one language against the other, informing the woman or your friend if you chose, otherwise keeping them in the dark. Yet you remained silent. On one hand you felt tied to Rich—we were schoolmates, the same age, had been together for a week of fiesta. But you had lost most of his candor, his ability to take nothing for granted. You also understood how a Spaniard could be led to take advantage of him; the unaware may bring out the malice in others. On the other hand you felt closer to Doña Claudia in her Mediterranean lack of innocence. Despite our differences in age, gender and country, you imagined that your Spanish great-great grandmother could have been a woman like her. In sum you were neither wholly American like Rich nor fully Spanish like her: something in between.

We walked down the stairs and into a light rain.

"What a lonely woman," Rich said.

"It got me when she teared up and talked about a family."

"Yeah."

"Doña Claudia's grown on me."

"Me too."

Until that day we had not seen so many people in the streets, so many brimming bars, cafés, trams, buses and taxis. Nor had we felt such exhilaration, tempered for a time by the exchange with our hostess. Even in the dismal weather the town had a vitality, a current that sparked like the wires of the electric tramways, like the barrages of fireworks crackling in every neighborhood. The air was cooler today, yet the mass of human bodies made it feel warm for everyone except your friend, the only person in short sleeves, who had goosebumps on his arms. You had offered him a sweater, but it was too small, and Rich refused to spend money on a new coat.

Horchata stands were already surrounded by customers. No longer shy, he ventured into the crowd and brought us two glasses of the grainy, ice-cold, almond-tasting beverage that slakes thirst as well as any drink. He had paid for both without hesitation. Rich was learning.

We walked from one barrio to another, looking at the tableaux, ducking into bars for a glass of wine with *entremeses* or appetizers. Recalling our landlady's words about paella, we decided to commemorate the birth of spring and St. Joseph's Day with the region's specialty. We hopped on a tram to the port, leaning out the door, the rain in our faces, one foot on the step, the other hanging out the side, laughing and shouting into the breeze.

At El Grao we did not see fishing boats being dragged on the sand by yokes of oxen as Sorolla has painted them, but a grey, white-capped sea and a brown beach strewn with storm-tossed seaweed. While waiting for a table at one of the countless eating pavilions, we drank beer and ate shrimp, cooked in garlic, and hot empanadas made from shredded fish, red and green peppers and pine nuts. Then we sat down to the main course, served on our table in its own *paellera*, the same charred, shallow pan in which it had cooked slowly over a wooden fire—the secret of a good paella—fueled with branches of orange and pine trees with their cones: firm, saffron-colored rice that sticks to a spoon turned upside down, fresh tomatoes and sweet peppers, mussels, clams, prawns, sea snails, octopus and squid. Doña

Claudia was right. In her honor we toasted one of many glasses of cold, white Valencian wine.

Rich wanted to pay the full tab. "We can split this one," you offered. "We've never spent so much on a meal."

"Don't worry, Eduardo, it'll all even out in the end." We both smiled.

"The rest of the night's on me, Ricardo."

"Then let's look for some expensive babes." We laughed with the conviviality that comes after six days of eating, drinking and carousing together.

It was turning dark and raining harder when we left the pavilion. Lightning slashed the sky. The storm, the fireworks, the throngs, the liquor and a feeling of anticipation made the city seem like an explosive lighted and ready to blow up.

Since we could not find space on a tram, bus or taxi, we hopped into the bed of a pickup. We could not have done it any other time of year: the rules of everyday life are suspended during Fallas. The driver and his two friends, packed into the front seat, smiled at us, giving the thumbs-up through the rear window.

When the streets clogged with traffic, we knocked on the rain-streaked window of the truck's cab, waved goodbye to the three Valencians and leaped to the ground. We stopped for a drink before heading to the heart of the modern city, the Plaza del Caudillo, Square of the Chief, named for the tyrant like the main square of so many Spanish cities. His cronies had defaced the center of town with thoughtless building and speculation, partly to punish it for being capital of the Spanish Republic during the war.

Fireworks burst against the gloomy sky. Walls around us reverberated, sparks rained down on wet streets. When we came to the immense plaza, enclosed by the tallest buildings in Valencia, the sound became so deafening that we had to plug our ears.

"The L.A. Fire Department would go berserk," Rich screamed over the din. "Some people must lose their hearing."

"The idea's to live as intensely as possible," you said in his ear, "to hell with danger. There are *pirotécnicos,* artists who do nothing else all year but design and make these fireworks."

"It's worth it, man." Another one went off: a deep, resounding blast echoed in the square while *tracas,* long strings of firecrackers, hissed and jumped along the tram wires and light posts. As the moist air filled with the smell of burning powder, we leaned back to watch the spreading, leaping, scintillating flowers of whites blues greens reds in the sky, falling slowly, dreamily through the rain as the crowd gasped, aahed, clapped in wonder.

"This makes fireworks on the Fourth of July look like sparklers," Rich said.

We followed the swarms of celebrants into a smaller plaza, where others were jockeying for the best spots to observe the *cremá,* the apocalyptic torching of floats at midnight. A band struck up the famous march, "Valencia, ta-túm-ta-túm-ta-túm-ta-túm-ta-tum-ta-túm-ta." Under our feet the pavement shook. By now we were all soaked and did not make the effort to seek shelter in doorways, under balconies, awnings, kiosks and trees. Not rain or anything else could spoil the fiesta.

We noticed men, women and their children eating fritters that were sprinkled with sugar. Those sweets appeared irresistible to a couple of Americans who were attempting to eat, drink and do everything like Valencians.

Standing next to us, a gentleman held a handful of the fritters for his wife and daughter. "What are they?" you asked.

He took a bite before answering. *"Bunyols. Es la costumbre—* you can buy them over there." The man pointed to a stall, covered by a colorful awning, where people stood in lines. *"Deliciosos!"* he exclaimed.

You turned toward your friend. "Ricardo, I think we need to try the bunyols."

"Always eat the food and drink the wine of the country."

We edged through the crowd to wait in line. It was your turn to pay.

Carrying our fritters through the press of people, we searched for an opening where we could watch the tableaux.

We approached a platform at a crossroads. When we were close enough to see the figures on its stage, Rich cried out, "Eduardo! Can you believe it—that's LBJ!"

We looked up and saw a caricature of Lyndon Johnson, some sixty feet tall. Dressed in a prodigious Stetson and cowboy boots, he sat on a pile of Vietnamese peasants, squashing them beneath a map of Indochina.

"Can't believe this!" Rich blurted. "They can do anything here."

"At least during fiesta," you said, sighting two *grises*, members of the Armed Police, in their inconspicuous grey uniforms, standing warily behind a row of palm trees. "And as long as the target is not the Spanish state, the military or the Church."

"I couldn't imagine a scene like that in the Rose Parade."

"*Jamás*," Never, you told him in Spanish, forgetting for an instant that he was American.

Although the rain continued falling, firemen arrived with hoses to douse façades, shutters and street signs, every inch of any surface that might kindle or flare in the coming holocaust. The *fallers*, whose title is untranslatable but plain enough in meaning, were preparing to ignite the float, urging the crowd to stand clear. They lit the corners with torches and jumped away just as the wooden frame, cardboard and papier-mâché caught fire. In a few seconds LBJ's gargantuan body and long-nosed, big-eared, grinning face had collapsed into the blaze, the force of the combustion blew us backwards, we shielded our faces from the heat as more tracas and rockets exploded, we heard the roar of the bonfire, smelled the burnt powder hanging in the air, tasted the smoke. As flames licked the President of the United States, you felt strangely empty, as though something inside of you, in your own past or nation was being engulfed, swallowed, purged there too. You recalled your other country, Mexico, also Khedidja in that moment when nothing was left but fire consuming itself, the sudden joy and loss, the craziness of it, a whole year, all of time reduced to a smoldering pile of ashes.

Falla in flames.

We saw other floats alight around us. Then Rich grabbed your left bicep, squeezing so hard that it hurt. (With a start you remembered the night when Gustavo had seized your forearm in Orizaba.) "It's him," he said between clenched teeth.

"Who?"

"Paco. That guy on the other side of the square in the black leather jacket—my jacket. Let's go get his ass."

You did not answer because Rich was already dashing across the plaza toward a dark young man who was strolling beyond the crowd on the sidewalk. The Spaniard did not see us: your friend had made a semicircle to close in from the blind side, moving with the feral grace he had shown when fielding a bunt on the baseball diamond.

"We got you, asshole!" Rich cried, clasping the man from the rear with both arms and lifting him off the ground. When you clutched Paco by his right shoulder, your friend released him from behind and caught him on the left side. Now we had him locked between us. The man appeared so stunned that he did not resist. He was big for a Spaniard and looked four or five years older than us.

"Whose jacket is that you're wearing, motherfucker?" Rich yelled. Paco remained silent, lowering his eyes. "And what about this white shirt?" Rich turned your way. "That's mine too." Again the man did not reply, looking uneasy but not terrified, almost as if he had been waiting for this to happen.

"Let's take him to the river, Ed," Rich stated with a confidence he had not revealed since arriving in Valencia. He was giving the orders now, like the starting pitcher, the team captain in high school.

We left the plaza, holding the Spaniard tightly between us. Moving among the debris of spent rockets and firecrackers, people had begun to disperse, heading to bars and homes after the cremá. Nobody bothered to look at us. We had been drinking so long, the Fallas had heightened our senses so much that we felt invincible, as though we could do whatever we wanted. At this stage nothing seemed to have consequences.

When a flash of lightning lit the sky, we could see Paco's face clearer: he had the olive complexion of Andalusian gypsies, an uncanny moonlight hue. Scars furrowed his cheeks, forming a complex pattern that resembled tribal markings. *"Ayúdame, Virgencita,"* he mumbled. "The Virgin can't help you now," you said in Spanish, "or God and all the saints." When Paco realized that you spoke his language, he started pleading. He was an orphan, he claimed, who supported his younger brothers and sisters in Córdoba. He had stolen Rich's clothes to help his family. Paco spoke with a thick accent of southern Spain, dropping and aspirating s's. As he implored with his hands, the leather of the jacket creaked.

His story sounded far-fetched. Here he was after all, wearing the stolen goods. Yet you felt a little sorry for him—he was so meek, so unresisting. Was that his ploy? You wondered, should Rich and I just take back the clothes and let Paco off with a scare? But the two of us had been rebuilding an old friendship of years, strengthened by the camaraderie of the fiesta; besides we had our whole male, American past behind us. There were too many bonds between us to desist.

As we drew away from the town center, Paco whispered out of Rich's earshot, "Your amigo's a *gilipollas,* a dumb ass. You and I could leave him and see the real life of Valencia." When he perceived the rage in your eyes, Paco changed his tactic again, imploring for pity, *"Por piedad!"* You ignored his words. Your silence must have frightened him more than anything you could have said. Meanwhile Rich looked determined, pulling hard, leading the way.

The barrios were not as well-lighted as downtown. Here or there an odd post stood with most of the bulbs burned out. We passed fewer and fewer celebrants. The streets wound, sloping gently, almost imperceptibly to the river. Something seemed to be tugging, drawing us down.

The dry bed of the Turia loomed in front of us, the old Guadalaviar of the Arabs, wide and dark as the night. (As your memories of Khedidja.) Keeping a close grip on Paco's arms, we climbed down the embankment. We steered him to the middle of the river bed, under the shadows of a stone bridge, where a trickle of water collected in a muddy pool.

"Let him go then stand behind him!" Rich directed. "Watch out Ed—the bastard could have a knife."

Both of us dropped our hold on Paco and leapt back. He was trapped there: he had you, Rich and the pool of water around him at equal distances. There was not enough light beneath the bridge to see the expression on his face.

"Take off the jacket, you son of a bitch," your friend commanded. Paco did not react, as though he had failed to understand. Rich repeated his words with signs and body language.

Hesitantly Paco removed the jacket, held it in front of him and waited for one of us to grab it.

"Go ahead Rich—it's yours."

"Nope," he said. Facing Paco and gesturing with his hands, he ordered, "Toss it here asshole!"

After delaying a few seconds, the Spaniard sighed and threw the garment underhanded to Rich, who set it on the ground behind him before stepping up to the thief. "Here goes!" he cried, rearing back with his right arm—his pitching arm—and swinging into Paco's gut. A thud echoed between the columns of the bridge, the Spaniard grunted, bent over and Rich caught him with a left hook to the ribs followed by a right uppercut that knocked the man's feet off the ground. Paco stumbled for a second but recovered, stood straight again, as if asking for more punishment. "Your turn Ed!" Rich screamed.

You approached Paco and spun him around. The thought that one day we might regret this streaked through your mind. As you raised both fists, they seemed leaden. You released your right arm. It felt like it was moving underwater, slowly, almost in a dream. The Spaniard's chest and his torso receded slightly with the impact: Paco knew how to yield to a blow while appearing to take it. Rich came around and grazed him with another left hook, then smashed his face with a right jab, making blood spurt from the gypsy's nose and mouth. You pummeled Paco in the stomach, the weight rose from your arms, something else driving them now, something to make up for the theft, for your friend's stolen clothes and money, the typewriter, for all the other Americans duped, cheated, betrayed by Europeans, all the Daisy Millers and the innocents abroad, New World against Old, New World avenges Old, no more innocence now, the Spaniard's body so flaccid that it offered no resistance to our punches and he slumped to his knees, fell into the pool, his legs submerged, his shoulders and head in the mud.

"Let's go!" Rich called, panting.

He picked up his jacket as we started loping toward the embankment, fearing we might have killed Paco, looking over our shoulders where he lay motionless in the pool. A few seconds later he was jumping to his feet as though nothing had occurred, shrieking "Hijos de puta!" and fleeing to the opposite bank. We stopped beneath a light on the sidewalk above the river. We had not noticed that it was raining again; cold drops were falling on our sweaty skin. Paco disappeared into the darkness.

"The fucker was playing possum," Rich said, out of breath, "just waiting for us to get far enough away for him to run. We must not have hurt him much."

"But we bloodied him to hell. Notice how he made his body go limp? He knew how to move with the punches."

"Yeah like hitting a ragdoll. You have to admit the bastard knows how to take a beating—he's probably been through it many times."

"He never tried to escape."

Rich's response seemed to come from far away, in a voice you had not heard before: "Nobody can escape what's coming to him." For half-a-minute there was no sound anywhere, the deepest silence we had known in a week.

When a faraway rocket sputtered, you asked, "What about all the scars on his face?"

Rich paused before replying. "Maybe from knife-fights. He was carrying a switchblade in Madrid."

"Wonder why he didn't pull it on us."

"Here's why," Rich said. From the inside pocket of his leather jacket he withdrew a black sheath and slipped a knife from it. "Why do you think the son-of-a-bitch wanted to hand us the jacket instead of tossing it?" Rich pushed a button that released a six-inch blade. It gleamed in the light from the post above our heads. "He would have cut us to shreds with this."

Your hands were trembling. "Reminds me of fights after school."

"Except it wasn't much of a fight. All we have to show for it are the jacket and these hands." We looked at our bleeding knuckles, then raised our eyes and caught each other's glance, where we saw a mixture of shame and pride. Everything had the clarity that comes after physical violence or making love.

"Rich, why didn't you take back your shirt?"

"I couldn't stand to have it touch my skin." Your friend surveyed the river and the embankment. "Ed, we should get out of here. I wouldn't be surprised if Paco called the police on *us*."

By instinct we followed the Turia away from town, toward the river's mouth. Occasional revelers were still holding forth in the outskirts. Through drizzle or rain we walked, feeling the letdown that comes after a fight, a game or match. Verses in Spanish kept running through your head: *"Nuestras vidas son los ríos / que van a dar en la mar..."* Our lives are the rivers / that empty into the sea ...

When we reached the coast, we were safe for the moment. Lightning flared in the lowering sky. We collapsed on the sand of the beach and watched the sun rise over a dark, stormy sea.

Part Three

Another World

11. Botín

After living in Franco's Spain, the California of Reagan and Nixon's America did not feel too strange. You served in the army, found a career, married, became a father, divorced. You would not have missed these years for anything in the wide world, yet nothing shaped you like those early trips to Mexico and Spain. In our teens and twenties we make the sharp turns in our lives. Later we take curves if we're lucky, a straightaway to the end if not.

When you returned to Spain in the spring of 1980, it had changed as much as you. The dictator was dead. A democracy had been born. The nation seemed vibrant with energy and conviction.

Young women embodied the new Spain. Instead of lowering their eyes as before, they stared right back at you, knowingly, without curiosity or bashfulness. They walked with their hair swinging around their neck and shoulders, swaying their body, making a breeze as they passed. (You inhaled their scent.) They were never still. In their movements you could discern their release from forty years of repression. Standing alone, they looked impatient, shifting their weight from one leg to another, jutting out a hip, an elbow, smoothing their shiny hair, smoking a cigarette in a challenge to men and the whole society. Standing among friends, they gestured with their hands and arms, laughing, pouting, frowning, rasping their j's or *jotas*, talking so loud in their hoarse voices that they would have been considered unfeminine in other countries. There was a tension, a feeling in the air that they were women, they knew it, you were a man, and what were you going to do about it?

Madrid appeared to be a new city in a different nation. Swelling like a wave in the capital, the cultural tide of *la movida* surged into

133

the provinces, renovating art, music, film, design, fashion. Life in the streets became more open. Rather than hiding in doorways and dark alleys, couples kissed and hugged in plain view. Armed police were almost as visible as before, but they were shielding the fragile democracy from unredeemed fascists, we trusted, instead of persecuting ordinary citizens, as the grises and the Guardia Civil had done for Franco.

The city found a leader for the occasion. Enrique Tierno Galván, known affectionately as the "old professor," presided over town hall from 1979 to 1985, six of the most crucial years in its long history. Perhaps for the first time Madrid became worthy of its ancient title as "capital of all Spains," the heart of a country that had shown the world how to cast off tyranny without spilling blood, a model for other nations, especially in Spanish America. Tierno created a new genre of public discourse, "the mayor's banns," pasted on walls throughout the metropolis. In them he chided or praised his fellow *madrileños* for neglecting or fulfilling their civic duties, always addressing them with fondness and irony. "Madrid has more than 40,000 waste cans, which are used very little," he observed in one of his pronouncements. Three days after the military's failed coup d'état on February 23, 1981—Francoism's dying gasp—Tierno would tell the city and the country in classic prose: ". . . The neighbors of this Town and Court wish to display in public their rejection of the recent violent acts that defame its prestige and stain its virtues . . . Long live Freedom!"

If Madrid found a mayor, the nation found a king. Without the decisive action of Juan Carlos I, people knew, the armed forces might have seized the government and halted the move to democracy, setting the country back by forty years. Some Spaniards, who were opposed to monarchy in principle, said they were now *juancarlistas* if not *monarquistas.* So the royal institution and the thwarted military adapted to the times. The third power inherited from fascist Spain, the Catholic Church, had not renounced the privileges of the dead regime.

Burning stages like a rocket, Spain was shooting from a dark past into bright, unknown space. Emigrants and exiles, who had fled to find work abroad, returned home, bringing their new hopes with them. Only five years after throwing off the shackles of despotism, the country had made itself one of the most open, prosperous and stylish in the world. Tierno Galván declared proudly, in words that could apply to all Spain: "Foreign voices call [Madrid] the center of happiness and the joy of Europe."

Before long you looked up your old friend Rodrigo Serna. Of course he wanted us to celebrate our reunion at Botín. Passing through the rickety door felt like entering a cool, moist cave. Antonio González, whom you had met years before, received us as though we had been there yesterday. It already felt like home.

As we ate our lunch of suckling pig, Rodrigo reviewed how he had finally married his girlfriend, how they had bought an apartment, had twin daughters.

"Why have you been away so long?" he asked.

"Hombre, you know how hard it is to travel with a family. It's even harder without money."

"Remember how you talked about living in Spain someday?"

"Yes," you answered yearningly. "But if I moved here I'd never see my son."

"Bring him along—it would be a great experience for a young boy."

"My former wife would never allow him to leave the country." Rodrigo looked puzzled, but you did not elaborate. It would have been too hard to explain the intricacies of child support and visitation to someone who lived in a nation where divorce was still a crime.

A few days later you returned to Botín in order to interview Antonio for a book. He stood behind the counter, talking to a group of customers. He smiled at you and made the fluid gesture of hand and arm that means *"Un momento."*

You walked to the cone-shaped tile ovens that had not changed since Antigua Casa Sobrino de Botín was founded more than two-hundred and fifty years ago. As he placed a cochinillo in the oven, held on a long wooden plank, the chef glanced up to greet you, *"Buenos días."* Logs of evergreen oak for the fire were stacked on the worn tile floor. It was the perfect hardwood for cooking meat slowly, burning evenly without flaring up or charring the pork, beef or lamb.

Botín.

Antonio walked around the counter to shake your hand. His smile brought you happiness always; it was one of the finest you had seen, generous and unassuming, traced by sadness. Followed by a waiter, we ascended the creaking steps. The main dining room on the second floor was crowded and noisy.

"I have a spot in the corner where we can talk later," Antonio said. He indicated a small table. "In the meantime go ahead and order your lunch here, Eduardo."

You sat in a plain oak chair. In his starched white coat, a spotless napkin folded neatly over one arm, a waiter recognized you from the lunch with Rodrigo. Like most of the staff he was older, perhaps sixty, having been with the house for years.

"The usual?" he inquired as if you were a regular.

"Claro que sí."

You observed the room: mighty beams on the ceiling, antique sideboards, walls of white plaster with rows of Talavera tiles, wrought-iron lanterns and dark oil paintings, chiefly still lifes. Most of the wood in that room and others at Botín appeared to be oak—not evergreen but the preeminent Castilian tree, strong and rough-hewn, full of gnarls and buckles. Between the walls and ceiling the junctures looked askew.

Your waiter brought a tray with a carafe of the house's tinto and a pitcher of water, beaded with sweat. Without food the Valdepeñas tasted thin. When Antonio sent up a plate of jamón as an appetizer—the rubiest, most tender ham in Spain—the simple wine came into its own.

For a first course you ordered *espárragos trigueros,* wild young asparagus served only in the spring. Antonio arrived and took a seat at the table. He was wearing a cream-colored suit that made his blue eyes look lighter.

"Are you going to have something?" you asked.

"My camareros eat before we open but I wait until closing. I will accompany you with a Scotch and some jamón."

He must have already spoken to our waiter. In less than a minute the man was serving a glass with two ice cubes and a bottle of Johnnie Walker on a silver tray.

We raised our drinks, saying "Salud!"

"In the beginning," Antonio said, "he would sit over there because the light was good." With a subtle motion of his brow and eyes he indicated a table across the room. It stood next to one of the small, fortress-like windows facing Calle de Cuchilleros below; an air conditioner filled the lower pane. An enormous, pink-faced man was sitting alone there, slurping baby clams from a terracotta bowl, dropping the empty shells in a pile on a plate.

"Ernesto used to arrive before we opened, around noon," Antonio continued. "He would ask for a bottle of wine, spread his books and papers on the table and work until his friends arrived for lunch. In those days hardly anyone would eat before two or three o'clock."

"What years were those?"

"Mid-twenties. I was just a boy. Ernesto told my father he was writing a novel whose last scene would take place at Botín. It must have been *The Sun Also Rises*."

"That scene ended up being the next-to-last."

"Yes but my father never knew this. He did not read books."

The waiter served the roast suckling pig, a golden quarter of a three week-old cochinillo that covered most of the plate, garnished by a single, roasted new potato. The pork's skin was still crackling from the heat of the tile oven. The meat was so tender it could be cut with a fork.

"Buen provecho," Antonio said before returning to his story. "I remember one day when Ernesto asked my father about his daily routine. This must have been in the 30s before the Civil War, because I was already a student. My father replied that he got up at seven in the morning and went to market, returned here and cleaned the meats, fish and vegetables, fired up the oven and waited for people to come for lunch." He paused to answer a waiter's question about something or other. "After closing the restaurant at five or later," Antonio resumed, "they used the kitchen to make fried Castilian pastries like *pestiños* and *bartolillos* because we needed the extra money—the restaurant had only twenty-one tables at the time. My mother and father would knead the dough with their own hands and elbows. So we ran a pastry shop until we opened for supper around nine o'clock. The last customers did not leave until two or three in the morning."

Antonio sighed and took a sip of Scotch, as if the story of his parents' workday had fatigued him. "When Ernesto heard this, he told my father in Spanish: 'Emilio, you work like a man in the time of Dickens.' My father asked, 'Quién es ese señor?' Who is that gentleman?"

We both laughed. The suckling pig and the Valdepeñas had begun to yield their bliss. Another waiter approached our table and whispered to the *padrón*. Two regular customers downstairs were vying to pay their bill, Antonio explained.

"The one who makes the reservation for the table has the right and obligation to pay," he asserted, sounding like an oracle. *"Eso es sagrado,"* That is sacred.

Our waiter served another carafe of Valdepeñas. The wine made you recall the scene in *The Sun Also Rises* where Jake dines with Brett at Botín and consumes five bottles of wine almost by himself. Not to mention the three martinis each drank before lunch at the fine old bar of the Hotel Palace. You asked Antonio about the five bottles.

"Probably an exaggeration but not inconceivable. The wine in that novel is not there by accident. It is almost a sacrament—Ernesto knew the natural, uninhibited man could emerge through wine. That is what he was seeking, what he found in Spain."

"The wine in the novel's Rioja Alta, right?"

"Of course."

"Why? Most of your customers drink ordinary Valdepeñas instead of more expensive vintages."

"Normally expensive wines would not be ideal here, Eduardo. Our fare is essentially the food of the Spanish peasant."

"Prepared with the skill and care of haute cuisine."

Antonio narrowed his eyes, and a humble smile formed on his face. He ended his thought: "But the lunch between Jake and Brett was not normal."

Your host excused himself to rise and say goodbye to the wife of the German ambassador to Spain. His father may not have read books, but Antonio spoke English impeccably and had learned French, Italian, Russian and German by himself.

When he returned to the table, you were finishing the main course. "Eduardo," he said, "I would recommend a light salad after the cochinillo. It is too heavy to digest well on an afternoon like this." You had forgotten about the warm spring day outside. Botín is like a cavern that envelops you, a place all its own, remote from the Madrid of cars, pedestrians and smog. Yet in some ways it embodies the best of the city and the country, its architecture, its food and wine, the hospitality, the deep sense of tradition. Botín contains the full richness and bounty of the earth, rivers and seas: Castilian lambs, pigs, veal, beef, sausages; green beans, asparagus and strawberries from Aranjuez, the garden and orchard of central Spain; sheep and goat cheeses from La Mancha, cured hams from Extremadura and Andalucía, trout and cheeses from Navarra; Mediterranean squid and langostinos, Biscayan hake and eels, Galician mussels, clams, oysters. As Rodrigo had said some fifteen years ago, Botín remained one of the great restaurants in a country that was a paradise of good food.

When Antonio took his seat again, you asked, "What do you remember about Hemingway during the war?"

"That was the only period in my lifetime when we had to close the restaurant."

"Rodrigo told me you've been open without interruption since 1725."

"Pues, let us say we were closed to the general public because we could not have served them. But so long as we had provisions our best clients could always find a meal here." Antonio hesitated before speaking again, as though he were remembering. "I see a massive figure, unshaved, wearing a leather jacket and a pistol strapped to his belt. He would stop by for a drink and talk with my father. 'Emilio,' he would say, 'do not worry about these bad times. After the war many Americans will come to Botín and make you prosper.' We had to wait two decades for that to happen, but his prophecy came true. He gave me the impression of a man who could see into things and change them with the power of his work. I was just a teenager at the time but already Ernesto reminded me of a person who knew exactly what he wanted and how to get it. He was acting and dressing and talking as he imagined was appropriate for a hero of those times."

Always attentive, Antonio noticed your empty salad plate. "Would you like dessert, Eduardo?"

"*No, por Dios.* I couldn't eat another bite."

"A *copa* then?" You smiled assent. Antonio beckoned a waiter.

"Ernesto would have been a good general or guerrilla leader," he picked up again. "Even a politician, if he had not been a writer with the obligation to see many sides of a question. He had a way of inspiring loyalty that I have not seen in any other man. Perhaps because he gave you the feeling that he would give his own life—on the spot—for anyone or anything he considered to be right. Eduardo, I would have done anything for him."

A waiter came with another problem for Antonio to solve. They spoke in low tones. You could not understand them. When the man left, your host explained. "It is about an old friend of the house who has been widowed. She has to make her living as a tour guide now. She is with an American couple who expect her to pay one-third of their bill. I told the waiter to have her jot a *garabato*, a squiggle on the check to make them think she is charging her share."

"Who pays for her?" you asked, feeling chagrined by your compatriots' ignorance of the Spanish code.

Antonio looked surprised by your question. "The house, naturally. She and her husband were regular customers for twenty-five years. One must help friends to maintain their dignity."

The waiter had brought a bulbous snifter heated over a flame to the temperature of the human hand. He poured out the caramel-colored brandy, Duque de Alba. You held it to the light, swirled it, breathed in the fumes rising from the glass, tasted. Spanish brandy will never be cognac, but after suckling pig and two carafes of Valdepeñas at Botín, it did not matter.

The drink warmed your throat. "Antonio, I've been thinking that Botín was sort of a querencia for Hemingway. It was one of the few places that didn't change in Madrid or anywhere else in the country. What made him keep coming back for almost forty years?"

"You have said it—because it did not change." Antonio's smile had something wise and wistful about it. "And speaking with modesty, as the Italians say, he kept returning because the food and wine were good. He knew they would not be compromised. He knew that we were open seven days a week the year around, that he would always find us here and be served a good meal."

"What's your schedule nowadays?"

"We still open every day of the year—for both practical and symbolic reasons. It takes so long for the tile ovens to cool down and heat up that it would make no sense to shut them down."

"So the fires are always burning at Botín?"

"Yes."

"I find comfort in knowing that."

Antonio smiled. "Therefore I do not have to explain the symbolic reason." His eyes moistened, and he paused before resuming his story. "Ernesto felt comfortable here because he was in *su casa*. We lived on the top floor in those days. You must understand, my friend—this was a house as well as a place of work. My family no longer live upstairs but in many ways this remains a home for me. My older son Antonio is already learning to host the restaurant. And his children will be the fourth generation of González's at Botín."

A big group of American tourists filed out of the dining room, led by their Spanish guide, a small, dark man who looked like an Arab.

"Antonio, you know how much I love Botín. But one thing bothers me—there are so many foreigners here, above all Americans. When people travel as a group, they act collectively and must be treated that way. The personal bond between client and waiter, customer and owner—what you hold dear—it's mostly lost. The sense of duty, the respect, the feeling of reciprocity, all that breaks down."

Antonio was too much a gentleman to make unflattering comments about his patrons or your countrymen. So you added, "This is the heritage of Hemingway too. He was one of our best writers and our best tourist."

"Al buen entendedor, pocas palabras," A word to the wise is enough, Antonio said.

The customers had left by now. You looked around the room. White napkins still draped ritually on their forearms, waiters were setting tables for supper. Except for the air conditioner in Hemingway's window, nothing remarkable had changed in this room for a half a century. Only the men and women who had come or gone or stayed. You were happy; it was hard not to be content when you dined at Botín. The happiness, you knew, was due largely to the people who had a livelihood there, Antonio and his staff, but it was also related somehow to those who had been here before, to the wine and the sacrifice of all those lambs, pigs, calfs, steers.

Beyond the thick walls and windows was Madrid, waking from its siesta, going back to work. You looked Antonio in the eyes. We both smiled.

He escorted you down the stairs to the ground floor. Before leaving you glanced into the kitchen, where the air around the tile ovens shimmered with heat, their firewood glowing inside. You had a sense that you were nearing the center now, the city's and the country's incandescent heart.

12. Alberto

Some things you remembered from earlier trips, like the need to find a headquarters, a querencia in the literal sense. After a week in Madrid you found a bar with a striped green-and-white awning, tucked away on a short street a few hundred yards from the Puerta del Sol. "El Patio" had good light, fine drinks, food and coffee. There was also something old-fashioned, provincial about it, so different from the glassy, modern cafés that were springing up all over the city. Walking through its doors was like arriving in southern Spain: the bar specialized in sherries, Cruz Campo beer, cured Andalusian hams, fried fish and gazpacho.

"What part United Estátes you from?" the barman asked in heavily-accented English. He served your drink at the counter.

By this time you could pass for a native speaker. Nobody else had identified you as an American or even a foreigner. You challenged the man in Spanish: "How can you be so sure I'm American?"

He placed the tip of an index finger below his right eye in the old Mediterranean gesture, pulling down on the lid. "Nobody fool me," he answered, smiling. He was about your age, perhaps a little older, with a dark mustache and a build like a Miura bull's.

Alberto. GONZALO DE LA SERNA

You sipped the sherry. "Alright I'm from California. From El Pueblo de Nuestra Señora La Reina de Los Ángeles," you intoned, recalling Concepción.

"What about that!" he cried in his gruff smoker's voice. "I live in California ten year—Los Ángeles, San Pedro, Sacramento, San Francisco." He pronounced the sanctified names of those cities as if he were speaking Spanish. "I have *restaurante* by Fisherman's Wharf in San Francisco."

"What kind of restaurant?

"What kind you think? Espánish, the best."

"Why did you leave?"

"The heart it call me back," the man replied, the palm of his right hand on his barrel chest. Then he pointed to the underside of his wrist. "My blood Espánish—like his." He indicated a large photograph of Curro Romero, the veteran bullfighter from Sevilla, hung on the wall in a prominent place behind the bar, where an image of the Virgin of Guadalupe might have been posted in a Mexican cantina. Silently you read the dedication: *"Para Alberto Flores, mi amigo sevillano de 'El Patio'. Curro Romero."*

"You're Alberto?"

"Sí Señó', pa' servirle," At your service. His Andalusian dialect sounded as strong as his foreign accent in English.

"My name's Eduardo." Touching your wrist, you told him, "My blood's also Spanish—some of my ancestors were from Spain."

"*No me digas, hombre.* But you still look like gringo." Alberto extended his right hand, big as a bear's paw, with thick, hairy fingers. We shook. During all those years in California he must not have learned to offer a firm handshake.

Pointing to the photo, he asked, "You see Curro in bullfight?"

"Once in Mexico. He was a coward with his first bull and divine with the second."

"That right, that how Curro Romero *torear.* He fall in mud or he touch sky. You like that Tío Pepe?"

You took a last swill of the straw-colored sherry. "Yes."

"That also why I come back to Espáin. Very difficult find *jerez* like this in America."

You would have preferred to speak Spanish with Alberto. His English was so weak that it hampered conversation, reducing it to the level of his plain vocabulary, abrupt sentences and broken syntax. But when you looked around and saw the other clients, all locals, you realized that he must have little opportunity to practice English here. Anyway his patois was so colorful that you decided to go along.

"I'll have another Tío Pepe."

Alberto took a black bottle from a refrigerator and pulled the cork. He filled your *copita* again, the glass shaped like a narrow tulip to capture the sherry's fragrance. "Now try these," he said, placing a white dish on the counter, full of oval-shaped berries with long stems. "My friend he bring them in truck especiál for El Patio, only bar in Madrid you eat them fresh—no can, no bottle."

When you tried them, you recognized a distinct taste. Seasoned lightly in olive oil, they were much larger, chewier and more flavorful than bottled capers. "Very good, hombre."

"Best *alcaparras* from Andalusía this spring. Now you take drink Tío Pepe," Alberto advised with a gleam in his brown eyes, like a parent telling a child to open a surprise present.

Gently you swirled the sherry in your glass, inhaled the perfume and sipped. The wine brought out the lingering taste of oil and capers on your tongue. Alberto seemed to be enjoying the experience as much as you.

"Good as a *verónica* by Curro," you said.

Alberto let out an explosive laugh. "Now you understand why I come back to Espáin. In America no fresh alcaparras, no Curro Romero. Also I live few blocks away, walk to work here—could not do in San Francisco." He served another dish of the bright-green berries. "El Patio only bar in Madrid all food from my *patria chica*," he boasted, touching his breast as he pronounced the Spanish term for a person's native region or homeland. "All my workers from Andalusía too." Alberto turned toward the other end of the counter. "Paco!" he called to a middle-aged man cooking something on the grill. *"Trae al caballero una' croqueta' de pehcao,"* Bring the gentleman some fried fish balls.

The cook's name brought back the memory of your last trip to Spain—another Paco from Andalucía, the young gypsy who had stolen Rich's clothes, money, suitcase and your typewriter. In the last fifteen years you had remembered, dreamed, brooded about beating him up in the river bed of Valencia. You did not feel good about it, but you had come to accept it as an irrevocable part of growing up. You also hoped that somewhere, sometime, Paco might have pardoned us.

That was long ago, and the sherry had begun to rise in your head. The world was starting to look as good as it always looked after wine and tapas in a Spanish café with the midday meal ahead.

The cook brought a plate of hot croquettes. This Paco must be about the age of the first one now, you thought—if the gypsy's still alive. *"Muy caliente','"* the man warned in dialect as thick as the owner's. You let the steaming, breaded fish balls cool for a minute before trying one: crisp on the outside, hot and creamy on the inside.

"Bacalao," Alberto said proudly. "How you say in English?"

"Salt cod."

"I remember now. Pay fortune for these when live in San Francisco, imported from Espáin and Portugál." He fondled one of the whole, dry salted codfish that hung on the wall by the cured hams. They resembled small, flat, white guitars. At least that's how they looked after two Tío Pepes.

"You wait try something better," Alberto urged, knowing an easy touch for food or drink when he saw one. "Paco! *Un plato de arro' con bacalao pal señó!"* A dish of rice and cod for the gentleman!

As Alberto filled your glass again, he asked, "You know Andalusía?"

"A little."

"Why little?"

You hesitated before answering, "I have more friends in Castilla." It would have been too complicated to tell him that you had spent time in the south but preferred other parts of the country. Tourism and overbuilding had ruined many places on the coast and the interior of Andalacía, where life often seemed too picturesque, too much like the Spain of *"charanga y pandereta,"* brass bands and tambourines, a great poet had said. A few months later, after you had come to know Alberto well, you could have told him, "I don't need to travel in the south—I can find it right here at El Patio, talking to you."

More customers entered as the pre-lunch hour drew closer. It was that time in a Spanish day when the world splits into two types of people: those who've slept late and are still taking their coffee, or those who've risen early and are beginning to order their apéritifs.

A tall, lithe young woman walked through the door, opening a path of awe before her. As she perched sidesaddle on the stool next to yours, she revealed two dark legs that tapered to thin ankles and small feet, shod in a pair of black stiletto heels.

Alberto swooped in like a torero for the *quite. "Sí Señorita."*

"Un cortao," she said drily, speaking from her chest with the harsh voice of so many women in Spain. Her black hair gathered the light and glistened as though she were standing in the sun. The other clients, all men, had stopped conversing to stare at her. She was one of those women who are so beautiful that your ribcage hurts to look at them. You could not help recalling Khedidja.

Just as Alberto brought her coffee, prepared in a demitasse with a touch of frothed milk, Paco served your dish of smoking rice that reeked of codfish. It was a collision between the late-morning and the early-afternoon cultures of Spain. The dark woman looked askance at your plate, lifting her cup and raising her nose as if to hold her breath and say, "Your food is spoiling my coffee," before drinking it off in three short sips. Then she rose from the stool, straightened her skin-tight skirt, muttered *"Adió'"* and undulated through the doorway amidst a silent wonder, taking every pair of eyes with her.

"Me cago en Dio'," I shit on God, Alberto cursed for all of us. *"Qué gachí!"* What a piece! All of us, each mother's son in the café knew a life without that woman was bereft. "Why didn't she pay for her coffee?" you asked.

Alberto leaned over and whispered, "She lover of UCD minister," using the initials of the Unión de Centro Democrático, the political party in power during the transition to democracy. "Offices upstairs," he confided, "twenty-four telephone lines. They make me good business—charge everything, pay big bill end of month." Alberto took a croquette from the grill, saying, *"Qué no haría yo con una mujé' como ésa!"* What wouldn't I do with a woman like that! He popped the fish ball into his mouth, chewed, slurped his fingers. "You doan have *mujeres* like her in United Estátes. *Pata fina y ojo' saltone'."*

Still reeling from the woman's presence, you were astonished by his words: it was the same expression Concepción had used a quarter-century ago, modified by Alberto's vernacular. In spite of all its regions, countries and dialects, at bottom the Spanish-speaking world is mostly one. You're lucky to belong to it, you thought with the blur or the clarity born from alcohol.

"Alberto. A friend from Mexico once told me the same thing about women."

"They understand about the women in Méhico. I live there three years—Ciudad de Méhico, Guadalajara, other cities. They also know about the horses and the bulls like Espániards." Alberto followed with one of his universal truths, no less lapidary for violating the rules of English grammar: "Where best bulls and horses, there best women too." You suspected how Spain's new feminists, waking from four decades of Francoist slumber, would react to his words. "Like Sevilla, *capital de Andalus*ía," Alberto continued, pointing first to the photo of Curro Romero, then to the stool where the brunette had been. "She *sevillana,*" he added. *"Ay, qué mujer!"*

"I heard the accent."

"You know Espánish o.k. Maybe your ancestors from Espáin they *andaluses*."

You didn't respond to Alberto's speculation, somehow believing your Spanish forebears probably came from Castilla.

New customers entered, old customers departed, some stayed. Slowly the memory of the woman's apparition faded from the room. You were curious to know more about Alberto, whose vitality had already won you over.

When he approached again, you asked, "Where else have you lived besides Mexico and the U.S.?"

"You name it I live—Francia, Alemania, Austria, Suiza, Australia. Work on ship as sailor. How you say, *marina mercante?*"

"Merchant marine."

"But I get tired of ocean and be mechanic for cars, own body shop near San Francisco, next be cook, save money, buy *restaurante*." Alberto spoke in barrages of words that reminded you of the *tracas* in Valencia or the bursts from a machine gun. His language seemed to contain a raw, combustible energy.

"Why did you leave Spain in the first place?" Paco had returned to clear your empty dish, replacing it with a second order of hot rice and codfish.

Your host waited for his employee to leave. He made a twirl of the hand, saying "*Buenóóó*" in the Spanish way, meaning That's a long story. "I have twelve brother and sister," Alberto resumed. "When I young no work and hunger of the *carajo*." He noticed my almost-empty glass. "You need another Tío Pepe, amigo." He no longer inquired what you wanted to drink or eat, anticipating his client's needs like a master waiter.

As you started on a third sherry, more people arrived. Alberto was too busy to pursue our discussion for the moment. Nearly all the customers were male, middle-aged, well groomed, dressed in tailored suits. Overhearing their conversations, you realized they were mostly all politicians who worked upstairs. You looked around the bar and thought about Alberto, his past, the years of hunger, travel and labor that had brought him to El Patio, where he tended the managers of modern Spain. It was an old tale. Poor men, largely from Andalucía and Extremadura, had crossed the seas in order to seek their fortunes in the Americas, then returned as *indianos*, colonists from the Indies, local boys made good. But Alberto's story was also a new one, because this Spaniard had not accumulated wealth from the toil of natives like many of his ancestors, nor did he come back to live the rest of his years in luxury and idleness, disdaining manual work and assuming airs of gentility.

You had feasted on enough food and wine to skip lunch. When you ordered a double espresso for the road, Alberto asked, predictably, "You not have comida today?" An explanation would have been futile. No matter how many tapas and pinchos one had eaten before lunch, it was heresy to miss the inviolate meal around which the whole day revolved in Spain. Bemused, Alberto shrugged his shoulders.

Serving your coffee, he asked, "You play tennis?" By this hour most customers had departed for the sacred repast.

"Yes—how did you know?"

Again he made the gesture of tugging on his eyelid. "You have *raqueta*, Eduardo?"

"At my pensión."

"You want play few sets this afternoon?"

"How about tomorrow? I've had too many drinks."

Alberto laughed. "I mean Espánish afternoon, five-six o'clock. You have tine—how you say?—*echar siesta*."

"Time to take a nap. Alright."

"Come back here we go to courts together."

"What time?"

"Whatever tine good for you." Suddenly you realized that Alberto's speech recalled somebody's from long ago. As we exchanged *adioses*, it came rushing back: the hawkers on the Avenida de la Revolución in Tijuana. Both he and they were men who had learned English on the streets, not in books or a classroom.

You walked to the hotel, slept off the wine, changed into tennis clothes and returned to El Patio. Alberto, dressed in a warm-up suit, introduced his wife Evelyn, an attractive young Salvadoran. (In this too he was like some indianos, who brought home a spouse from the New World.) He left her in charge while we departed for the subway. Spain's athletic insurgence had already begun, but it hadn't taken hold. Passengers on the metro stared at us in our warm-up suits and tennis shoes, our rackets and sport bags slung over our shoulders, as though we were visitors from another universe. We descended at a station in the Casa de Campo, the former royal hunting preserve that had become a municipal park. There the city had built asphalt courts on the rolling land where the siege of Madrid had been fought during the Civil War. Since tennis had been a sport for the rich under Franco, usually played on a clay surface at private clubs, public courts remained a novelty. But nothing was free here; the city charged an hourly fee. An elderly attendant wearing a *boina* or beret, a man from the old Spain, took reservations. Players slipped him a *propina*, the tip that makes things work in this country.

Your new friend secured a choice court partly shaded by a hill, pine trees and evergreen oaks. While Alberto began to stretch, you opened a fresh can of balls: the aluminum top snapped, air escaped in a pop.

"That beautiful sound," he said. "Only one sound better—opening bottle *champaña."* This match held promise.

As we warmed up, Alberto swung hard at the balls, going for a kill on nearly every groundstroke, an ace on every serve. What he lacked in finesse he made up in power, like the fighting bull he resembled unmistakably. The balls sounded solid on the asphalt, echoing against the low hills around us, with the mountains, the Guadarramas in the background, the serried skyline of Madrid on the other horizon.

"You see those tennis balls?" Alberto shouted as we rallied. He jutted his chin toward the other courts. All the players seemed to be using faded balls that had lost their weight and fuzz, bouncing wildly without the satisfying resonance of newer ones.

"Tennis still expensive for people," Alberto huffed, charging the net. "Espáin country of naked tennis balls and cojones," he guffawed as he put away a volley. You tried to make the return but were laughing so much that you fell to your knees.

The rules at the Casa de Campo did not permit customers to hold a court beyond an hour. But Alberto had bribed the old attendant so that we could play as long as we wished. After three and-a-half sets you noticed a faint tinkling noise. It sounded so distant, so muted that you paid no attention at first, guessing it could be your imagination or fatigue.

When we changed sides between games, you asked Alberto, "Am I hearing things? What's that sound?"

He threw his racket in the air like a player who's just won the finals at Wimbledon, roaring laughter. "What wrong Eduardo, you never see *ovejas* and *cabras* when you play tennis in America?" Alberto pointed to the hill above our court. Among the live oaks and small pines you saw black-and-white shapes of sheep and goats, their heads low to the ground as they fed on grass. Through the late afternoon breeze came the muffled music of the bells around their necks.

Alberto explained: the city contracted shepherds for one month a year in the spring before their flocks migrated to the mountains for summer pasture. The animals had free forage in the Casa de Campo, where they kept the grass and weeds low, also devouring trash left behind by madrileños, who still had not learned to clean up their litter. Alberto thought it was an ingenious solution, almost as effective as the tractors and riding mowers in American parks, less wasteful of fuel and more pleasing to the eye and ear. With our white tennis clothes, our rackets and modern paraphernalia we stood there, bare tennis balls bouncing dully on the courts beside us, oh Spain, listening to the soft counterpoint of shepherd's bells.

"This nothing, nada," Alberto said, waking you from reverie. "Every *otoño*—how you say it?"

"Autumn."

Unable to pronounce the word, Alberto frowned and repeated the Spanish: "Every otoño the sheep they come downtown Madrid— "*coño, la mihma Puerta del Sol!*" He swayed his head and chomped his teeth like an animal grazing grass. "Nobody can stop them. *Nadie,* not even army or police."

Your friend described how the country's *Mesta,* the association of cattle farmers and shepherds, guarded the time-honored right to lead their flocks through towns and cities. In Alberto's presence those clashes between the new and old in Spain seemed to multiply. He had lived on the extremes of both worlds, and with a natural, unschooled intelligence he perceived their incongruities.

We walked back to the metro, at ease and tired after splitting four sets. Alberto pointed to a delicate almond tree in white blossom, sure sign of a Madrid spring. "Me and brothers eat those flowers after *guerra*"—the Civil War, he meant. His lexicon did not extend beyond the words necessary for survival in English. "We also eat *corteza*— how you say?"

"Tree-bark."

"Also like dog," he added with a canine woof, appearing amused but slightly embarrassed too. Before you could react, Alberto exclaimed in his normal, thunderous voice, "Now I invite you drink beer eat tapas and pinchos!" He pointed to a little outdoor café with tables under a pair of twisted evergreen oaks. A hand-painted sign hung over the low roof—"El Almendro," The Almond Tree.

Standing at the bar, we drank cold beers with a round of appetizers: wedges of Spanish omelet, slices of bread with Manchego cheese made from ewes' milk, *toreras* or marinated olives and onions speared on a toothpick, kidney beans cooked with blood sausage and chorizo. Alberto struck up a conversation with the owner, a middle-aged Castilian who attended customers. His wife, a tiny woman in the rear, barely visible from the counter, did the cooking.

"Did the gentlemen have a good match?" the man inquired, using the third person out of respect for us.

"Sí Señó,'" Alberto replied. "You're lucky to be so close to the tennis courts. I own a bar downtown—have to take the metro here." "I'm too old to play," the owner responded, "and I'm from the *campo.*" Although he looked like someone in his early 50s, about ten years older than us, in a sense the man was profoundly right: the members of his generation and his social class, los pobres y humildes, could not have dreamed of playing tennis in Franco's Spain.

"And what about you, Señora?" Alberto called to the wife, who had already been captivated by your friend's exuberance. He knew that this lady, dressed in black with a scarf over her head like the women in a thousand Spanish towns and villages, would no more play tennis than fly a supersonic jet.

She smiled with resignation by the stove. "*Todo lo que no sea esto de guisar no lo sé hacer,*" I'm no good at anything but cooking.

Those words broke your heart but not Alberto's, who told her, "The way you fix beans with morcilla and chorizo, Señora, you don't need to play tennis." He smacked his lips. "You can come to work for me any time. Bar El Patio, Calle Arlabán, two steps from the Puerta del Sol."

As we drank, ate and talked with the lady and her husband, you considered how the country had changed since the Civil War, since Franco's days and your first trip to Spain some fifteen years ago. Enjoying the bounty available to nearly everyone today, we were standing on the ground where thousands of soldiers had died in the defense of Madrid. A poor boy like Alberto, born in the late 1930s or early 1940s, had eaten tree-bark and flowers as a child; by the 1980s he was playing tennis, once the sport of the rich and well-born; he ate as well as any man in the world and owned a successful bar frequented by politicians who ran the state. On the other hand many Spaniards, not much older, like the couple who owned El Almendro, still had not moved fully into the present. The two countries, ancient and modern, lived side by side.

Alberto pulled a wad of bills from the pocket of his warm-up suit, paid the check and left a crisp 100-peseta note for a tip. When he was younger, he must have lived by his wits and cunning like the gypsy Paco, you guessed, recalling again the young man who had robbed Rich so long ago. Now this Andalusian, Alberto, was your companion. Somehow his friendship helped make up for the other thing, but how could he or anyone else understand?

If we had met a few decades earlier, you thought, we might have gone carousing together instead of playing tennis. It would have been fun to go de putas, whoring with Alberto, as you had done with Gustavo. But that kind of initiation was vanishing in the wake of sexual freedom and AIDS, not to mention that our youth had gone too.

Alberto also brought Concepción to mind. Like your old friend he was salt of the earth, the Spanish earth, the Old World instead of the New. Unlike Chon, who would never escape the wasteland of the border between the U.S. and Mexico, Alberto, after fleeing abroad in the dark years, returned home to thrive in the young democracy. He could stand for the Spain risen from the wreck of war, the misery and oppression, you thought, as we walked back to the metro. The fascists had won the battle in the Casa de Campo, the war also, but in the end they had lost the country. When we reached the station, the first stars were shining above the hills.

Whenever you travel to Madrid, you stop at El Patio to see Alberto, have a drink and taste the dishes he offers for the occasion. You'd be less inclined to seek out your early comrades from Mexico— Concepción, Lolo, Laura. Those friends and teachers must be old by now, in their sixties or seventies, if they were alive. A younger man like Zanahorio might have changed so much that we would have little in common, you feared, and both of us would have been disillusioned. It's better to leave those memories where they belong, inside our heart and head. There they can grow or fade and die.

With Alberto it was different. We met each other late enough in life to renew our bonds at any time. When you drop by El Patio to see him, he rarely allows you to pay for the drinks and tapas. Someone must pay, because the bar looks crowded at peak hours, before lunch and dinner. Video games flash and beep in the corner, but the food and wine are good as ever. Anyway it all seems the same after your first glass of wine in the long Spanish morning with sunlight streaming through the windows and the smell of codfish frying on the grill.

13. José Mari

At noon on Sunday, the sixth of July 1980, the fiesta exploded. A big rocket whizzed from the second-floor balcony of the Town Hall. As it hissed, leaving a trail of white smoke, the crowd in the plaza and streets held its breath. The rocket hung over us in the washed sky, it burst and the feria had begun. For nine days and nights there would not be a moment of silence in Pamplona.

It felt the way we used to feel when the bell rang on the last day of school. Now we had a full week of fiesta ahead. It would hold as much life as a whole summer and a lot more death.

"Eduardo, welcome to San Fermín!" José Mari cried, smiling from ear to ear, his pale blue eyes smiling as well. We embraced. He stands 5'6" tall, has a perfect bald head, a beaming face that brings joy to anyone who sees it.

José Mari. GONZALO DE LA SERNA

We pushed slowly, inch by inch, through the crush in the Plaza Consistorial, the heart of Spain on July sixth of every year. José Mari appeared to know almost everyone in the city: he could not advance more than two or three yards without meeting somebody who recognized him. He hugged the men, kissed the women on both cheeks, Spanish-style, lifted the small children in his arms. Some of his male friends rubbed the smooth, irresistible crown of his head.

When the crowd got too thick for us to walk through the alleys, we stepped into a tavern for a snack, a drink and rest. Others must have had the same idea; inside it was teeming and loud as the streets. José Mari knew the bartender of course, so he managed to secure a glass of red wine for you, a *mosto* or unfermented grape juice for himself. He was the first Spaniard you'd met who did not imbibe.

As we tried to find a spot with enough room to lift our glasses, you asked, shouting above the din, "Do you feel pressure to drink, especially during the feria?"

"Ya lo creo. It can only be compared to the nagging of Spanish mother-in-laws for their sons and daughters to have babies."

"I guess you didn't withstand that pressure so well."

He laughed, "Not with four children—so far, at least. As for wine my friends gave up on me when they saw that I'm as wild as them *without* alcohol. I get high on people."

The young men around us, unlike José Mari, needed wine to feel the elation. Refusing to let the fiesta catch up with them, they were already on their way. Older men, veterans of many Julys in Pamplona, looked unhurried as they eased into the festivities, bracing themselves for the long days and nights. They knew that pace meant everything here, whether you were drinking, eating, dancing or running the bulls. There was so much more to come.

When José Mari started to pay for our drinks, the bartender told him they'd been covered. He pointed to a bearded man in the corner, seated with a group of friends, who smiled and gave the thumbs-up. Always some of the most generous people in Spain, the *navarros* or Navarrese become all the more lavish during the Sanfermines.

José Mari spoke in your ear to make himself heard. "Let's go because I can't remember that guy's name."

Since it was lunch time, the streets had almost emptied for the one daily lull: not even the feria can stop Spaniards from sitting down to a three-course meal. The women are the ones who make it possible, keeping everything on track—shopping, cooking, tending the children, washing and ironing clothes for their husbands, sons and brothers who are spattered every day with spoils of the fiesta. They also take pleasure in the celebration, but they must pay a higher price, sleeping still less than the men.

When we reached José Mari's apartment, you hugged Pili and the kids, three boys and one girl, who ranged from fifteen to five years old. In your honor the paterfamilias brought out a bottle of Navarrese red. He uncorked it and poured a glass for you. His middle son Alberto, just eight years old but already straining to prove himself, wanted to taste it too. (You suspected he would become as spirited a drinker as your friend, his namesake at El Patio in Madrid.) José Mari allowed him a very small glass. He was training the boy for San Fermín and for manhood.

We sat down together to a first course of *alubias pochas* from Sangüesa, a nearby town known for its fresh white beans, followed by *cordero al chilindrón* or lamb and red pepper stew; a salad of watercress, onions and olives; *batido de limón*, a kind of lemon freeze for dessert. Drinking that wine, eating that food, surrounded by the noisy warmth of a Spanish household, you recalled your failed marriage and your own son, who was exactly young Alberto's age. How right it would be to have him here, for both of us to feel the presence of a family again. Like José Mari you had reached the stage when most men are husbands and fathers. There had been years for being footloose, wandering, exploring, seeking the unknown. Now it was time to lead a different sort of life, one that divorce had taken away from you. For the moment all that mattered was to live the fiesta and leave the rest for afterwards.

During the sobremesa Pili rose, left the dining room and returned with a large shopping bag. "A gift from San Fermín to you, Eduardo."

You opened it to find a full outfit for the fiesta: the classic shirt and pants of white cotton, a red silk kerchief and sash for neck and waist; white, red-laced espadrilles with rubber soles.

"They'll turn black with dirt in a day or two," Pili said.

You thanked your friends, took your gift to the bathroom and changed. When you came back, Pili and her daughter exclaimed, almost in unison, "You're a real *pamplonica* now!" Following the habit of centuries, they were clearing the table while the men and boys digested their food and smiled at your new clothes.

Leaving his wife and kids behind, José Mari led you to the Plaza Consistorial, where the *chupinazo* or rocket had ignited at noon. The sun shone bright as it can only shine at four-thirty of a summer afternoon in Pamplona's mountain air. Again people jammed the square and the balconies of buildings around it. The city fathers, dressed in tuxedos and top hats, some of them smoking postprandial cigars, were preparing to lead the entourage in the procession from the plaza to the church of San Lorenzo, where they would pay homage in solemn vespers to the martyr St. Firmin, the city's patron.

As usual in Spain there was another, secret rite beneath the surface. The *mozos*, the young men of Pamplona, would dance the traditional *riau-riau* ahead of the official cortege, delaying it as much as possible in the parade to the church. The longer the procession lasted, the more time they would have to raise hell and get soused on the route. It was also a matter of establishing, right from the start, who was in charge of the feria—the authorities or the people. In the new democracy of post-Franco Spain the officials barely stood a chance.

When the band struck up the riau-riau, women and children left the square. It was one of many male rites in the Sanfermines. Singing and dancing, the mozos headed the line, followed by the entourage: a cordon of navy-uniformed police between them and the marching band, whose members also dress in white; the city fathers in formal black; the eight loping, bobbing *gigantes* or giants, each supported by a man in a wooden frame concealed under long, bright-colored robes; in the rear the *cabezudos* and dwarves with oversize heads of papier-mâché, the buffoons and harlequins of San Fermín.

You imitated José Mari in the opening steps of the waltz, guided by the banging of drums in the dark, Arabic-like refrain, then turning, gliding as we lifted our arms above our head, our hands dancing as much as our feet to the happy, lilting melody, all of us smiling at each other in the exhilaration of the festival begun, singing the defiant chorus:

> ... *Porque llegaron las fiestas*
> *de esta gloriosa ciudad,*
> *que son en el mundo entero*
> *¡una fiesta sin igual!*

We made the final, double leap to the sharp Basque words "riau-riau!" and it resumed again, time after time in the world's longest, slowest parade of five hundred yards.

We moved from the plaza into the Calle Mayor, the sun beating on us, the heat trapped and the music reverberating between the walls of buildings as we exuded clean sweat, so unlike the anxious perspiration of workaday life. It's really true, but nobody believes it who has not been at the feria with the men and boys of Pamplona.

After each four or five repetitions of the refrain the band took a break, we shouted *"Agua! Agua!"* to the spectators on the balconies above, who cooled us by throwing down bucketfulls of cold water and ice more heavenly than holy water. When people on the sidewalks offered us botas, we held up the leather bottles with extended arms, threw back our head, and the wine hissed into our throat. We squirted each other, our white pants and shirts stained red, ducked into the taverns to slake our thirst fast before reclaiming the street to prevent the cortege from gaining on us, to push forward in this struggle to see who could control the procession and the feria.

While the band played again, you stood with José Mari in the street, leaning against each other, too tired to keep up with the 20-year-olds. For a moment you were both inside and outside the fiesta, close enough to feel the percussion of the band, the quick stepping of the dancers' feet on the cobblestones and the male-voiced song, distant enough to see it whole now with the young men bobbing up and down with raised arms, the musicians blowing and thumping their instruments, making the ground shake, the gigantes gliding in their circling, floating dance with wide-open eyes and all at once you felt the power of San Fermín, knowing it didn't come only from the music, from the people or their saint but also a force rising out of the earth from a long, long time ago.

San Fermín. RAFA RIVAS

You did not live in Pamplona, you were not a Navarrese or a Spaniard, yet thanks to José Mari you were a part of the celebration now. You were forgetting about your marriage, divorce and loneliness, your own past, all of them driven away by the dance, the music and crowds, cleansed by the water, wine and sweat. And you realized that it must also work for the other men who were jostling, encircling and embracing you, perhaps for their women also, their mothers sisters wives lovers daughters, those girls and ladies looking down at us with smiles from balconies and windows, who had their own, different San Fermín.

We held off the band, the police and the city fathers until 8:20 that evening, setting a record for the number of times the song was repeated (one hundred and eighty-one). Tempers flared among the officials because the religious service was two hours behind schedule, and scarcely anyone had been able to attend the *novillada,* the novice bullfight that afternoon. While José Mari returned home, you walked to the hotel for supper and a nap. You had never danced four straight hours in roasting sun and cool shade on streets of cobblestone.

After a late supper we met more friends at midnight, mostly couples in the spacious, tree-lined Plaza del Castillo where we danced on sore feet until three in the morning, trudged to a park for a neighborhood fair, danced more, limped back to the main square to drink a free cup of soup offered to everyone, found an outdoor café and ordered hot chocolate with *churros* as dawn broke in Pamplona. Sitting at our table under the trees in a fresh breeze, we heard the thin, faraway sound of the *txistus,* the Basque fifes that play the early-morning *dianas* or reveilles to the accompaniment of drums before the running of bulls. After you've heard it once or twice, you'll remember that music always. It will pierce your heart.

There we said goodbye to the ladies. For the third time in less than twelve hours we walked to the Plaza Consistorial, crossroads of the festival. Your friend did not want you to try the *encierro* yet: "Just get a feel for the streets, the runners and the bulls," José Mari advised. "The first day might be unlucky." In fact several men would be wounded that morning. None died. The bad luck would come later.

We ate the customary breakfast at Casa Marceliano: *magras con tomate y huevos*, fried eggs and rashers of lean ham in a spicy tomato sauce, a matchless dish to revive yourself after a day and night of dancing, to restore strength after the exertion of the encierro. Then José Mari walked home while you returned to the hotel and collapsed into the sensuous late-morning, early-afternoon sleep, the longest stretch in bed during a full day and night of feria.

You took the main meal at the Maisonnave, one of the best hotel-restaurants in Spain: *langostinos* from the Bay of Biscay, big as small lobsters; alubias again, leading to *marmitako*, a fisherman's stew of bonito with red peppers in tomato sauce, all of it washed down with a chilled rosé from the Navarrese vineyards of Señorío de Sarriá; cuajada or sweet curded milk for dessert; coffee; *pacharán*, the Basque liqueur, rounded off in the sobremesa by a cigar from the Canary Islands. Already you were learning that one of the secrets of San Fermín is to eat often and heartily in order to stay awake through the night. The food—nearly all of it fresh, not canned, frozen or packaged—must also supply Pamplonicans with the energy to celebrate so hard on such little sleep.

Leaving the hotel, you strolled up the tight Calle Jarauta, more an alley than a street. Like a bullring it was divided by a clean line between sun and shadow. (Spain, country of *sol y sombra*.) You stopped at the makeshift bar and headquarters of Peña Anaitasuna, one of the eating and drinking societies that rule the city during the festival. The club's band was beating drums, tuning horns and fifes, unfurling the fifteen-foot banner it would carry on its march to the plaza de toros.

You spotted José Mari and his close friend Rafa. We embraced. They wore outlandish hats in contrast to the sober traditional costume. José Mari sported an old Robin Hood cap cocked to one side with a scraggly, fallen feather, Rafa a gigantic, foam-rubber Mexican sombrero at least four feet in diameter at the brim. The band struck up a song, and we followed the peña's swaying banner down the narrow street to the bullring.

Older people, mothers, children watched again from balconies, waving as we passed. During Sanfermines everyone, not just José Mari, seems to know each other. For one week the city's remaining social and political barriers almost collapse. Your friend pointed out a former member of ETA, the radical group for Basque independence, who was dancing a *jota* with an official of the more conservative PNV, the Basque National Party. As we reached the square in front of Town Hall, we could hear the other peñas approaching with their pounding songs and music.

A couple of teenage boys squirted us with a *sifón* or flit gun. They seemed to know José Mari and Rafa. The soda water refreshed us in the bright sun. One of the dwarves with a gigantic head, called "*Caravinagre*" or Sourpuss, whacked us with an inflated pig's bladder on the end of a string. Some kids took revenge for us by swatting him on the backside as he was looking the other way. You were learning about this playful punishment that you must take and dish out in Pamplona.

A boy approached us, holding a necklace of garlic in one hand, an open bottle of perfume in the other. You wondered if he knew us, maybe from the riau-riau, where we had met so many dancers. Wavering on his feet, he smiled and held his offerings to your nose, asking, "*Cuál te gusta más?*" Which do you like better?

"*El ajo,*" The garlic, you told him without hesitation. He responded, "*Sí!*" laughing and hugging you. There is no place for perfume in the streets during San Fermín with the good bracing smell of sweat in the air.

We came out on the shady Paseo de Hemingway, full of cars, tourists and white-dressed mozos singing and dancing toward the bullring, banners rippling above them.

"We have forty minutes before the corrida," Rafa said. "Let's stop by Hartza for a while."

He grabbed José Mari by one arm, you by the other, pulling us down the Paseo, past the big stone statue with foreign boys and girls perched on the writer's monolithic, bearded head, down the hill and across the tree-lined avenue to a modest building of two stories. We walked up the stairs to the landing, where we passed a little brass sign with "Hartza" engraved above the figure of a bear.

Rafa cracked the door to peek inside. "They've already closed," he said, "but I see some clients in the dining room."

He dropped to his knees, motioning for us to do the same, like a platoon leader going into battle with troops, and the three of us were crawling toward the kitchen, singing "La Cucaracha":

> La cucaracha, la cucaracha,
> ya no puede caminar . . .

You were right there with them, yet you could not believe it. Two middle-aged businessmen, married, with kids, had the freedom, a sense of the absurd, the fiesta spirit of life to become like children. No matter what their age, the members of the eating and drinking clubs are called mozos because they're youths at heart for one long week of every summer. This must also keep them younger during the rest of the year, you grasped with certainty now, creeping forward on hands and knees..

You tried to think of a parallel in American life, conjuring up friends who might be similar to José Mari and Rafa, but you could not picture them crawling, singing "La Cucaracha" in front of the customers and the three sisters who own the restaurant, who were smiling and summoning cooks and dishwashers from the kitchen to come and see, the late diners at their tables joining the lurching Mexican song between sips of coffee and pacharán or puffs on their cigars. Then we rose to our feet, the sisters coddled us, saying, Give me an abrazo and taste this besugo, Try this sea bream prepared in a sauce of parsley and garlic, Do you have a smoke, Take this Havana, and we were kissing and hugging the women and saying goodbye, running down the stairs and up the hill, bumped by dancers from the peñas as we drew near the bullring.

José Mari stopped for a second in the street, paused and looked at the treetops. *"Aquí la vida es vida!"* he cried. We did not know if he was addressing us, himself, the trees or the cosmos.

The other members of the Anaitasuna were waiting for your friend to pull his annual caper before the first corrida. They explained that José Mari bought an *abono* or subscription for the whole fiesta but refused to tender it, preferring the challenge and the triumph of entering without a ticket. We watched him as he approached the turnstile, his arms spread-eagled and forefingers wagging back and forth in rhythm to his slow, bouncy steps, a joyous, beatific, all-the-teeth-in-his mouth smile on his face as he sang "No, no, no" to the ticketman, seeming to grow in stature before our eyes, all of us laughing so hard that we had to cry, even the policemen joining in on the fun. José Mari had crashed the gate again. It could only happen during San Fermín, these pranks, this breaking of rules, this good will among people.

The plaza de toros pulsated with songs of man-voices and music. Every group had its own band of fifes and drums, each trying to play louder than the others. We found places on the sunny side of the arena, reserved for peñas, wherever we could squeeze in. It didn't matter because nobody paid attention to the numbers on our tickets. If we had tried to take the seats shown on our stubs, we would have run the risk of being thrown out—or more likely, into the ring. We would not have been ousted by the police or the ushers but by the mozos themselves, the real and final masters of the feria.

If you sit on the sunny side at your first corrida in Pamplona, refrain from wearing clothes that will not be improved by showers of wine, sangría, champagne and beer, or by sprinklings of flour, bread, tomatoes and soup. In prosperous, post-Franco Spain the drink of choice is cava. As the bottles pop open, their contents spray into the stands. It's the best way to keep cool under a bright sun in the midst of the plaza's mayhem during San Fermín.

The figure of the *toro bravo* underlies everything in Pamplona between July 7th and 14th. It may not be a city for seeing the best bullfighting, but it's the one for seeing some of the best fighting bulls. San Fermín is the country's one major series named for them: Feria del Toro. More than esthetic grace the crowd demands bestial courage from the matadores, a raw bravery that mirrors the creatures' force and the power of the fiesta itself.

After the paseo or opening procession, Luis Francisco Esplá hurried through his capework with the first bull. He could not brake the charge of the wide-horned animal from the ranch of Conde de la Corte. With the *banderillas* he moved almost as far and quickly as Mexican and Venezuelan *maestros*, zigzagging in and out of the bull's terrain then driving the shafts down hard in the withers, the man's body straight, his arms stiff as the horns passed. Aficionados jumped to their feet at this display of valor, speed and timing. Esplá placed the second and third pairs of shafts close to the first, high on the animal's shoulders. After each set the mozos roared from the sun:

> *¡Como Esplá no hay ninguno!*
> *¡Esplá es cojonudo!*
>
> Like Esplá there's none!
> Esplá's well-hung!

(How could you forget Alberto's description of Spain as the country of cojones and naked tennis balls?) Hazarding a fine or suspension, Esplá took advantage of the public's mood, walked to the sunny side of the ring and dedicated the bull's death to political prisoners from ETA. No matter what he did in the last *tercio* or third of the corrida, he had won over the Navarrese with their sentiment in favor of Basque autonomy. A cheap trick—"*Demagogia!*" called some of the older spectators from their expensive seats on the shady side of the ring. Politics had invaded the arena and San Fermín, like everything else in Spain. But they could not ruin the feria.

Esplá failed to control the bull's charge or dominate him with the *muleta,* the smaller cloth of serge or flannel used in the *faena* or finale: no linking of passes, no "running of the hand" as the critics say. It almost looked as if his arms weren't long enough to make it calm, smooth and with emotion. He went into the animal with a strong thrust of the sword. The bull dropped. The plaza fluttered with white handkerchiefs demanding the award of an ear for Francisco Esplá.

After the third bull of the afternoon the clubs took out their meriendas of sausages, stuffed empanadas, omelets, giant bocadillos and *ajoarriero,* a specialty of San Fermín, salt cod cooked with oil, garlic, tomatoes and eggs. Many of the men and boys were too drunk by now, too unruly and busy eating to pay attention to the action below. One teenager yelled *"Cabrón, carbon, carbon!"* Bastard, bastard, bastard! at whatever *matador* happened to be facing a bull below, not even bothering to watch as he stuffed his mouth with a sandwich of fried eggs and sausage or doused his neighbors with a plastic squirt gun.

Esplá and the other two toreros, Paco Ojeda and Ángel Teruel, could not work their animals with enough skill or daring to recapture the public's fickle attention. Esplá had already cut the sole ear and won the day. His work with the banderillas had been brave, skilled and exciting, but it lacked the slowness, the depth, the mystery of the man and bull together in a great *lidia.* A performance that is mostly athletic does not give the feeling of tragedy. In the end it has something common about it.

When the main gate opened, the crowd spilled onto the arena, and you descended to the front row with José Mari and other members of the Anaitasuna. We jumped into the *callejón* that runs around the ring and nudged our way through the horde, following the track of smoothed-out sand and dried blood left by the dead bulls when they were dragged to the slaughterhouse.

Among all the citizens of Pamplona only José Mari and his friend Rafa, in accordance with a fortunate, unexplained privilege, were allowed to enter the sanctuary of the abattoir where the butchers did their work. The space brought to mind a tall, open garage or a small warehouse, where the temperature was cooler than outside. Already flayed and headless, the last bull of the afternoon hung upside down, his flesh still steaming, his carcass swinging open-legged from metal hooks. The other five in the lot had been butchered in turn. Their meat would be sold to the public. Meanwhile the organs of all six dead animals overflowed a wide concrete trough. A larger basin held the hornless, glass-eyed heads of the Conde de la Corte brothers who had been running through the streets of Pamplona, wholly armed and lethal, just twelve hours earlier. In another trough their horns lay wide-spread and point-lifted.

One of the big, ruddy Navarrese butchers, officiant of the prescribed immolation, wearing high rubber boots, set the mino-taur-head of the last bull on the ground, raised an ax and chopped the horns from the skull, splattering flesh, blood and hair on the closely-packed onlookers, held back by a chain, who did not flinch because their white clothes had already been soiled in the streets and the plaza. Then the man placed the creature's head and horns in their separate basins and hosed down the floor. A damp, sweet smell of blood, meat and organs filled the air.

Another butcher handed José Mari a sack heavy with the twelve testicles of the fallen bulls. The two men regarded each other with a look of reverent complicity, as Theseus might have regarded King Minos while showing him the slain monster's head. But when our friend whispered something to make the butcher laugh, slapping his thighs, we knew we were in Pamplona and not ancient Crete.

As we moved slowly with the mob, there was a good smell of sweat in the air again and a warm tiredness in our bodies. White ban-ners surged over our head, bands playing as we flowed like a stream under the trees around the plaza, chanting deep-voiced songs in the heat, dancing down the hill in the early evening to the town, where the bars had already turned on their lights.

The next afternoon Pili and the other wives prepared *cholas* or *criadillas,* a delicacy made with the bulls' testicles, served for the main meal. Two days later they fixed *estofado de toro*, a stew cooked with the braised meat of the animals killed on the sand the previous afternoon. As you ate those dishes, concocted in different ways with garlic, onions, herbs and red wine in compliance with the arts of Basque-Navarrese cuisine, each with a unique flavor, you thought about the encierro and San Fermín. Every morning the bulls gallop through the streets of Pamplona, inevitably wounding some men, at times taking victims. On the same afternoon they're killed by toreros in the arena, and their remains are sold at auction or given to friends, who cook and eat the flesh and organs. Life to death, death to life in a cycle that has not ceased for centuries.

San Fermín is a religious festival with a patron saint, but it also resembles a tribal feast whose celebrants consume their gods. After all the bulls descend from animals worshiped for millennia in the primeval world. Eating the slain creatures, some feel as close to the divine as when they take the Host at Mass, perhaps even closer. Those people do not invoke a complex theory of transubstantiation. The meat and testicles not only represent the body of a dead god, like the Communion wafer: they *are* his body. And what about the blood? Here the fiesta shares the symbolism of the Eucharist again: the chalice holds Christ's vital fluid, while the bull's blood matches the red wine that rushes through Pamplona like a river. Take it away and the Sanfermines would bleed to death. Remove the running of the bulls and the fiesta would be trivialized into a quaint amusement. Nobody dares admit the truth, but human as well as beastly blood completes the ritual, bestowing the dimension of tragedy. That year it gushed when we should have expected it, on the 13th of July.

By that time you had learned enough from José Mari and other friends to run the encierro on your own. Like nearly everyone else you had spent the night in the streets, drinking, eating and dancing. You wondered if your body would be able to respond without sleep, but in the cool air of first light, with the knowledge of action to come, you felt alert. Before going to the course, you returned to the hotel to change your canvas espadrilles, blackened and frayed by a week of feria, for tennis shoes.

The streets and the Plaza Consistorial smelled of early morning. Everything looked fresh in the new light. It was Sunday. Through the night more men and boys had been arriving from towns in Navarre and the provinces, filling the bars, cafés and streets. With more runners and less space to maneuver, the route would be treacherous. Most of the danger, as in the rest of our lives, comes from ourselves and other men more than the gods.

Balconies overflowed with spectators. People standing along the barricades offered us wineskins and bottles. When a drunk darted between the wooden planks into the street, tripped and fell on the cobblestones, policemen dashed to his aid and carried him beyond the fence. The mood of lighthearted, innocent camaraderie had become somber, as serious as the horns of the 1,300-pound animals who were waiting to burst from their corrals.

We warmed up by stretching and jogging in place. Our faces showed the restless anticipation: thinking about the bulls may be worse than running with them. The traditional prayer of San Fermín, repeated many times before the encierro, helped soothe feelings of isolation. Lifting our right hand, holding a rolled-up newspaper that would serve to mark our distance from the herd of racing bulls, we saluted the saint and appealed for his protection:

> *A San Fermín pedimos*
> *por ser nuestro patron,*
> *nos guíe en el encierro,*
> *dándonos su bendición.*
> *San Fermín, ¡viva!*
> *San Fermín, ¡gora!*

> We pray to San Fermín
> our patron saint,
> may he grant us his blessing

and guide us in the run.
Viva San Fermín!
Long live San Fermín!

As it had done for seven straight mornings now, the resonant, man-voiced song raised goosepimples on your arms. Where else in all the world can you hear thousands of males singing a prayer in unison, one they believe in truly, your own voice blended with theirs? There are no more atheists during the encierro than in the trenches during war.

Throughout the night these men had moved as groups, celebrating together. Now there was a mounting sense of loneliness as each mozo thought about the bulls who would come stampeding up the streets, faster than the speed of any human. Within a minute or two every mother's son would be by himself. Although they had been allowed to run for the last several years, not a single woman could be seen inside the barricades. The encierro, from the seven fighting bulls and six steers to the thousands of Spanish and foreign men along the course of nine hundred yards to the bullring, for the time being remained a masculine birthright.

A military band played a final diana from a street beyond the runway. Trios of players, two fifes and a drum, made the plaintive music that pulled on our heart. When they finished, we knew it must be close to eight o'clock, hour of the encierro, whose start is always punctual and its end always unpredictable.

The last minutes before the running of the bulls are the most eerily quiet in the week of fiesta, with their hush and low murmur, as though the city were holding its breath. You spit on the cobblestones for good luck. Also to test the old belief that you could not spit when really frightened. So much for that superstition: you were and you could.

Without warning, the first rocket exploded to proclaim the opening of the corrals. Your pulse raced, runners began to move, talk or shout to shake off the built-up tension. Seconds later another rocket went off to signal that the last bull had passed through the gates, meaning the whole lot would be galloping up the hill of Santo Domingo. Everything was happening like a shot, with such thrill and fear that it could have been a dream except that you were fully conscious, more awake than any other instant of your life. Loping across the large square of the Town Hall, seeing it decked with flowers and the flags of Spain and Navarre flapping in the breeze, you felt the awe of the moment, a dark knot in your belly. You moved slowly at first, jogging ahead of the others on the wide Calle Mercaderes, around the sharp corner where the bulls often slide and stumble, up the narrow Estafeta, the longest straightaway. Behind us the noise grew louder and more urgent, but you could tell from counting in your head that the bulls must still be well behind us, knowing you shouldn't let the throng's panic throw off your perception of time and distance.

Men were running hard now. You tried to avoid being swept away, going a bit faster, right up the middle of the long street that leads to the ring, looking over one shoulder then the other. Before spotting the animals, you heard a clatter of hooves on the cobblestones amidst the shouting and sensed a rumble of the ground, saw them coming quickly, tight as a herd, the black bulls with ivory horns and the creamy-brown steers scattering the white-and-red-clad men. Someone fell huddled on the sidewalk but the beasts paid no attention to him, driven by the bovine instinct to be together. They were gaining on us: nobody can outrun fighting bulls for long. Suddenly our troupe thinned out, a little area opened out as if cleared by the horns and you fell into that wondrous space, running at full tilt, feeling the joy and terror, vigilant but allowing your body to follow itself free, mouth dry, you could never spit now, heart pounding, you couldn't stay ahead of them longer, you jumped onto the sidewalk without losing stride and pressed into a doorway, watching them gallop by, big, heavy, muddy-sided, tossing their heads.

Animal smells hung in the air. A blond boy lay flat on his back in the street. Two white-suited men ran over and dragged him to a doorway. Then we heard shouts behind us. We knew something must be wrong, one or more bulls might have been separated from the herd, which must be well on its way to the ring. We heard cries of "*Toro rezagado! Cogida!*" A bull in back! Somebody gored! Minutes seemed to elapse in dread until we saw the animal detached from the others, alone, charging jerkily, head moving from side to side, turning backwards until a man with a cape lured him forward. Holding your back against the doorway, you saw the horns with their bossed cusps as the bull stopped to charge a boy, one tip stained and shining red down to the fat base of its curve, blood on his muzzle, dark little eyes with light circles around them, great hump of sinew on his neck, the force, his breath as he passed, horns swinging. You dashed behind him in order to reach the plaza before they closed the gate to keep the animals in the ring, spectators along the barricades and in balconies and windows applauding the runners, unaware of what could have occurred farther back in the route. We crossed the open square and entered the long chute connecting the course to the arena. As we reached the end of the runway, we saw the last bull go through, the big red gates slammed shut behind him, and we heard the voices of 20,000 people inside and knew that something grave was happening.

You grabbed the top of the gate, wriggled up and saw the chaos in the ring, too many men and boys on the sand where a fighting bull loped around with a striped sweater caught on his left horn. There was a loud cry and you saw a bearded man caught on the animal's right horn below you now, for so long it seemed, just ten yards away, he fell onto his back and the bull moved off, another scream of horror as viewers realized he had been gored.

The goring of Vicente Risco (center left). GÓMEZ

13. José Mari

Four mozos tried to lift the fallen one, but the beast spun and charged again, the crowd blocked your view, then you saw the toro thrusting swiftly and surely with its horns, left-right, right-left with the precision of a boxer's fists or a butcher's knife, lifting and shaking the man like a rag then dropping him hard, making you feel sick, the crowd groaning. The animal moved away once more, some mozos picked up the body of the victim, whose intestines dangled to the ground, carried him to the infirmary, hampered by the people milling on the sand.

All but two of the bulls had entered the corral at the far end of the ring, then the one with the bloody head remained alone, surrounded by *cabestros*, the ponderous steers with clanging bells around their necks. The toro bravo moved nervously toward the gate, a boy distracted him with a muleta in his hand, breaking the rule of never spoiling the animal for the professionals who must face it that afternoon in the formal rite on the sand. With wadded newspapers or their fists several men whacked the kid before the police took him away. Some foreigners in the audience objected, unaware that the boy's thoughtless action might lead to the goring of a torero. The bull reached the gate to the corral, made one more feint to charge, turned and entered the darkness with the lumbering steers. A final rocket went up, and the encierro had ended.

Later that morning we read in the papers that two men had been killed, more than thirty wounded. A normal run lasts less than three minutes. This encierro had taken ten minutes and fifty-five seconds from the first rocket to the last—one of the longest in the history of San Fermines. It felt twice as long.

The first fatality was José Antonio Sánchez, twenty-six, son of a farmer from the Navarrese town of Cintruénigo. He had been gored in front of Town Hall and carried forty meters on the horns of the bull who had been separated from the herd. They bore him on a stretcher to the Provincial Hospital, where he died after a blood transfusion of fifteen liters, the newspapers said. But how could that be true if a human body contains only five or six liters? At any rate José Antonio would not see another encierro. Even if he had survived, this might have been his last. He was scheduled to marry María J. Chivite on the 23rd of August, and young men often swear to their fiancées that they will not run the bulls after marriage. Some break their promise too.

The animal who killed José Antonio Sánchez was named Patirrota, Broken-Hoof, weight 522 kilos, number 55 from the ranch of Salvador Guardiola, Heirs. Out of respect for the dead man they hosed off the blood from the creature's horns and snout before he entered the ring to be killed by Tomás Campuzano as the sixth bull of the afternoon's corrida.

The other victim was Vicente Risco, twenty-nine. A bachelor, native of Extremadura, he had lived in a town of Navarre for twelve years. They said he had been training for a black belt in karate. He was gored by the last bull to enter the corrals, and he died three minutes after reaching the infirmary.

The animal who killed Vicente Risco was named Antioquío, weight 543 kilos, number 17, also from the ranch of Salvador Guardiola. He was killed that afternoon by the second Campuzano brother, José Antonio (christened like the first victim), in the same arena where he had impaled Vicente in the morning. Some people believed this bull had killed both runners. It happened with such speed and confusion that nobody will ever know for certain.

Nowadays Spaniards and foreigners wonder if a custom like the encierro can fit into the safe, modern world of the European Union. Each year more voices rise in protest against both the running of the bulls and the corrida. But if these two rites were forbidden, the Sanfermines would lose the current of tragedy that deepens and dignifies them. And the world would lose its most powerful fiesta, one that draws from our remotest past.

From time to time someone dies at Oktoberfest, Carnival or Mardi Gras, but those are accidents, not the ordained sacrifice of a fighting bull, the inevitable risk of humans being gored in the arena or the encierro. In Pamplona more than anywhere else one learns that death and life are like lovers who cannot reach plenitude without each other. San Fermín is truer to life because it's also truer to death, *ley de vida,* law of life. More faithful to the rules of a vital, mortal game.

The encierro can be a crucial part of a man's story. A boy raised in Pamplona begins by watching the spectacle from a balcony or behind a barricade, then runs with brave calves in a miniature version for children. Each year he tests his valor a little more, until he finally goes up against the full-grown fighting bulls about the time he enters puberty, discovers women and becomes a man. By running with the animals who embody the masculine principle, by getting close to the horns that can bring violent pain and extinction, he partakes of a collective rite. After being tested in the fiesta of life and death, he may return to the encierro and draw on the bulls' strength again. Later he can watch his sons go through the same initiation and renewal. Since women are now permitted to run, it may also become a focal part of their lives, perhaps in unexpected, illuminating ways.

In the case of foreigners the event may also be a decisive stage of their growth. For you it turned out to be a means of reaffirming your male self enfeebled by divorce, solitude and middle age. During those seconds by the bulls' horns you found a different kind of freedom, a new sort of elation, greater solidarity with your own sex, more confidence in yourself and others. You did not think about this during the fiesta but months and years later, over and over so many times that you know it's real.

As much as anything else the encierro shows the Spanish sense of time and history. The practice springs from ancient traditions, yet it requires us to live wholly in the present. It has a set of rules and regulations, a right and wrong way of performing each phase, but in front of the bulls' horns we may find the most spontaneous moments of our lives.

Since the last day of the feria, July 14th, fell on a Monday that year, fewer men tried the encierro. We had a clean run. After the carnage of yesterday, to race down the dark tunnel of the plaza de toros with those beasts behind you and emerge in the bright, open ring was like passing through the neck of your mother's womb into the light of the world. Afterwards we felt drained as if we had given birth to something too.

That also happened to be José Mari's day for working in the Anaitasuna's headquarters on Calle Jarauta, where members took shifts manning the temporary bar. In gratitude for all your friend had done on your behalf, in order to allow him more time at play, you took his turn for the afternoon and evening. After being a customer at hundreds of Spanish bars and cafés, it felt right to be on the inside of a counter, as if you had crossed another barrier in the fiesta and the country.

At midnight we walked to the Plaza Consistorial once more, where the feria erupted more than a week ago. The city looked as if it had undergone a siege. In the gutters between the cobblestone streets and sidewalks lay hundreds of wine bottles like the casings of empty bombs or artillery shells on a battlefield. The toes of the mozos' feet were showing through their grimy canvas shoes.

San Fermín had started with a bang and ended with another, smaller one: an explosion of tracas, the strings of fireworks you had first seen in Valencia. How far away the Fallas seemed—the papier-mâché floats going up in flames, Doña Claudia, Rich, thrashing Paco in the river bed. You were young then, an outsider in Spain but moving in, caught between it and your own country, as much an observer as a participant. Now in Pamplona you were older, still learning but surrounded by Spanish friends, living the fiesta alongside José Mari, Rafa and the others, the ones you knew and the ones you didn't. As more fireworks detonated, they lit up the Plaza Consistorial with memories of this spot during the past week: the rocket on the first day, the riau-riau, the running of the bulls each morning. All had intersected here, in this square, axis of the feria and our world for one long week in July.

As your reward for surviving from first to last, José Mari removed his red silk handkerchief, made a histrionic bow and offered it to you.

The Anaitasuna's emblem was sewn onto one corner of the cloth, showing the saint in the act of offering a benediction with his right hand, the words *"¡Viva San Fermín!"* embroidered below. Your friend tied the kerchief around your neck.

"You're an honorary member of the peña now, Eduardo," he said. Our companions watched in uncustomary silence. As you looked into José Mari's clear, light-blue eyes, tears ran down your face with beads of sweat. Never had you felt so Spanish.

Next the club's musicians handed you one end of their immense banner, your friend took the other and we started our last procession that year, a mock-serious funeral march to the tree-lined Plaza del Castillo and back to our bar on Calle Jarauta, carrying little white candles and lamenting in gloomy voices with everyone else,

> *Pobre de mí,*
> *Pobre de mí,*
> *¡que se han acabado*
> *las fiestas de San Fermín!*

> Woe is me,
> Woe is me,
> for now has ended
> the fiesta of San Fermín!

The feria did not cease, and there was still plenty of time for the fun we'd been enjoying all week, dancing jotas and pasodobles between stanzas of the dirge, seeing who could lie longest in the street like a corpse while the others sprayed him with wine, setting fire to trash bins overflowing with the refuse of nine full sacred reckless days. For the families of José Antonio Sánchez and Vicente Risco, whose sons had died in the encierro, the funeral was not in jest.

But the fiesta doesn't die, because you can go back another year. If you cannot return, others will, always. San Fermín will not end, because it comes from far down in the earth, deep in time, a place and its people. It will never die, because it brings so much life with the death.

14. Fernando

"We have a young bull reserved for tomorrow *a las cinco en punto de la tarde,* at exactly five o'clock in the afternoon."

"Not a good omen," you said, recalling the poem about the death of a bullfighter "at exactly five o'clock in the afternoon."

As usual Fernando could read your thoughts. "Do not worry, Eduardo—these rural *capeas* are not as punctual as formal bullfights. By the time we enter the ring it will be at least 5:30."

The extra half-hour seemed like a small reprieve. *"Gracias a Dios."*

Fernando smiled. "I am glad to hear a skeptic like you invoking Our Lord. There are no atheists in the bullring or in battle."

"Or the encierro."

"True," he acknowledged, rubbing his chin. You could sense the gears of Fernando's thought turning beneath his high forehead and grey temples. "But I prefer the art of toreo to the encierro, which is more like a sport."

"In which men can be maimed or killed."

"True again, Eduardo. Like skiers, football and hockey players and other athletes. In bullfighting injury and death are not accidents but necessities—always the animal's, sometimes the man's." He paused. "It is unfortuante that our capea falls on a Tuesday. We could not arrange it for any other afternoon." Fernando did not have to explain the superstition about the day of bad luck in Spanish-speaking countries, similar to Friday in the Anglo-Saxon world.

The black telephone rang on his desk. He waited for his wife or one of his daughters to pick up the call in the house's other wing. The women served as buffers between Fernando and the world of Madrid outside, where traffic hummed below.

A red light flashed on the telephone. When he picked up the receiver and spoke in a soft tone, almost inaudible—so unlike the raucous speech of many Spanish men—you surmised he was talking to a patient. And listening: Fernando's a rare individual who knows that it can be as much an art as speech. He's a good psychiatrist and confidant because of his capacity to hear what others say.

Sipping from your glass of amontillado, you walked to the far end of the study, where you sat on a leather divan used by Fernando's patients. Venetian blinds on the windows filtered the light of sunset onto the wood-paneled walls, the parquet floor and Persian rugs. In this apartment, four stories above the Paseo de la Castellana, Madrid's Park Avenue, one had the sensation of being in a realm removed from the city and its heat, noise and dust.

As Fernando talked on the phone, you faced the floor-to-ceiling bookshelves. There you saw framed photographs displayed between volumes on psychotherapy and toreo, in Spanish, French, German and English, some of them written by your host. Here was a shot of a youthful Fernando posing in the callejón between his father, the former surgeon at the bullring in Alicante, and Ernest Hemingway; an adolescent, passionate-eyed Fernando on the seashore, looking like a Mediterranean god; Fernando as a young man attired in a well-tailored *traje corto,* the suit worn to test brave cows and bulls on ranches; an older Fernando dressed in the same style, working a small calf with a muleta in his left hand and a sword in his right; a silver-haired Fernando in a black cape and sombrero; a middle-aged Fernando shaking hands in various photographs with Karl Jung and Domingo Ortega, with other toreros and men whom you did not recognize. Objets d'art were interspersed among the books, mostly statues of fighting bulls in cast iron, onyx, marble or bronze. On the other walls hung diplomas from universities in Salamanca, Madrid, Geneva and Zurich; sketches, oils and watercolors of bullfighting scenes, most of them painted by Fernando himself.

Fernando. GONZALO DE LA SERNA

He placed the phone on its cradle with a sigh. "Excuse me, Eduardo," he said in his Britannic English. He continued, switching back to Castilian: "A patient of mine is having another crisis. It seems his only relief comes from making love or cursing."

"Healthy outlets for anyone."

"But his wife is an old-style Catholic, Holy, Roman and Apostolic. She thinks the sole purpose of intercourse is procreation."

"Then tell him to cuss her out."

Fernando smiled. "I am afraid my own moral preferences may have interfered. I counseled my patient to curse less and urge his wife to make love more often."

"Why are you opposed to profanity? In the new Spain that's almost unpatriotic."

Fernando eyed the floor before responding. "Because I have always been a nonconformist, I suppose. During the Franco years I was one of the few Spaniards who defended psychotherapy—in my books, public lectures and my classes. Now that the Generalissimo is no longer with us and psychology, psychiatry, psychoanalysis and any kind of therapy is in vogue, I have come to doubt the value of my own profession." After thinking for a moment, Fernando added, "With Franco we could say whatever we wanted in private, but swearing and above all blasphemy were taboo in public. With the so-called transition to democracy it has become fashionable to curse everywhere. I refuse to follow the latest fashion in this or anything else."

"If people use foul language too often, it loses its power to surprise and shock."

"It has its appropriate time and place. Guess what one of my female students told me the other day at the university? 'Dr. Claramunt, you're my only professor who doesn't say *tacos*, dirty words in class.'"

You could not resist laughing. "Sorry, Fernando."

"Hombre, I don't blame you for laughing. 'Go ahead and use *tacos*,' she warned me, 'or you won't be popular with students.' That is pure demagoguery, Eduardo."

"You wouldn't want Spain to return to the dictatorship, would you?"

"Franco's state was authoritarian. But we had quite a bit of economic freedom—the government did not run the whole financial system like communists in the Soviet bloc. Nowadays we have more individual rights yet people have learned that democracy cannot make everyone happy." Fernando stopped when the muted sound of a collision reached us from the avenue. He made the sign of the cross before resuming, "So after the initial euphoria we are in a phase of *desencanto* or disillusion. One writer captured the country's mood when he called it *una fiesta triste*, a sad fiesta."

"That wasn't the mood in Pamplona a few weeks ago."

"Are you not glad I encouraged you to go?"

Before you could answer, there was a gentle knock on the door. "*Adelante,*" Fernando said. He looked slightly annoyed.

Pura opened, peeked in, scanned the room and pointed to your empty glass. "Eduardo," she said, "I see that Fernando has left you without sherry. We'll fix that soon." She had dark hair tied in a *moño*, a knot at the nape of her neck in the Andalusian style. She was several years younger than her husband. "It's time for both of you to stop talking and come to join us for entremeses before supper. You'll need nourishment if you're going to fight that bull tomorrow at Cortijo Bravo." Until Pura said those words, you had succeeded in forgetting about the event for a minute or two.

We followed her down a long hall decorated with more taurine paintings. We passed other rooms, including an alcove with a time-worn prayer bench, a Baroque prie-dieu that faced a wooden crucifix in the bloody Spanish style, almost lifesize. The space served as the household chapel. In Madrid, with the highest real estate prices in Spain, Fernando and Pura's house seemed like a palace. Comprising two flats joined into one, it occupied half of a full floor of this large building on the prestigious Castellana. When we sat around a table in the living room, where the family took informal meals, you felt a warm breeze from the windows of the main balcony and saw lights on the avenue, one of the city's longest, widest and most elegant.

Your hosts' daughters were helping to prepare the table. One, in her twenties, with dark shiny hair, resembled Pili; the other, seven years younger, with a fair complexion and blond hair, favored Fernando. As they served olives, artichoke hearts, Manchego cheese, jamón serrano and bread, it occurred to you that he was your first Spanish friend with nubile daughters. You envied his stable life at home, the dimension of the past felt in every corner of this house. Never would you be able to create a family as steeped in permanence as Fernando's and Pura's. Perhaps you really did not want that. Weren't you the one who had the freedom to visit them, not the other way around?

Fernando's mother joined us at table. Since her husband died years ago, Doña Remedios had worn black from head to foot. Her Christian name also belonged to the old Spain. She had been baptized in honor of the Virgin of Remedies, one of many incarnations of Mary embodied in women with names like Angustias, Consuelo, Dolores, Mercedes, Soledad, etc., a roll call of conventional female virtues like mercy and consolation or their expected lot of solitude and suffering.

When we had finished most of the hors d'oeuvres, Pura and her daughters served a summer dinner of gazpacho, tortilla española, salad and honeydew melon. Ignoring the next day for a while, you enjoyed the food, wine, conversation and the company of three generations. Fernando, the patriarch among his wife and daughters, treated his mother with the same deference owed him by the other women in the house. After all it was the older generation whose memory grounded the family in custom and the past. At José Mari's and Pili's apartment in Pamplona nearly everything had revolved around the kids. Here one had a deeper sense of time and tradition.

As the man of the house Fernando was in charge of wine. He had selected a bottle of Rioja Alta from his cellar, a 1970 Marqués de Murrieta Castillo Ygay, which had been breathing on the table for the last two hours. After drinking the first glass of the brick-colored wine, we were situated squarely in the center of Madrid, Castilla, Spain and the universe.

During the main course Fernando asked you for the saltshaker. Picking it up and extending it in one hand, you noticed a malicious smile on his face.

"Never do that!" he warned, and you realized it had been a test. "*Es mala suerte,* Bad luck, Eduardo." You returned the shaker to the table, looking sheepishly at the women around you.

"*Papá,*" said his oldest with a tone of mild remonstrance, "don't torment our guest."

The paterfamilias was undeterred. "Observe, Eduardo. Merely place the shaker on the table where I can reach it, like this." As he demonstrated, you noticed Fernando's hands—small, immaculate, white. They had never washed a dish or cooked a meal in their fifty-plus years. You wondered how many centuries of female subservience had been required to make possible such a pair of hands. But you also remembered that they had fought bulls with cape, muleta and sword.

Fernando swirled the Rioja in his glass. Smiling, he said, "You are probably thinking we are irrational. Many people believe the constant danger in the corrida makes bullfighters sensitive to good or bad omens."

"Are they right?"

"Perhaps. But we are not superstitious, Eduardo. It is just that certain actions bring bad luck." Fernando laughed while his mother assented with her mantilla-covered head, utterly serious and addressing you, "*Sí señor.*"

As a cool breeze from the sierra billowed the curtains of the balcony window, both daughters cleared the table. Doña Remedios retreated to her room.

During the sobremesa Pura served us tall glasses of *paloma,* anisette mixed with ice cubes and water. We watched the transparent liqueur turn cloudy and acquire the color of a white dove's wing.

It was eleven o'clock, an hour when Spaniards may call their friends after dining. On cue the phone began to ring. Writers, critics, breeders, toreros young and old called Fernando to discuss the latest news of bullfights celebrated that day: we were in the late-summer season of ferias and festivals. As your host conversed, he sipped his paloma and followed the highlights of the day's corridas on TV with the sound turned off.

Pura, always attentive to her guests, must have noticed your uneasiness. "Eduardo," she started in her serene voice. "Are you sure that you want to go to Cortijo Bravo tomorrow?"

"No. It's Fernando's idea."

"Don't let him drag you into it. He has experience that you don't have, could never have in America. He's been fighting capeas ever since he was a boy."

The expression of disapproval on Fernando's face showed he was listening to Pura, even as he continued drinking, talking on the phone and keeping an eye on the television. You took long swills of your pale paloma, trying to let the alcohol distract you from thoughts of Tuesday afternoon.

Fernando hung up the telephone, rose from his chair, turned off the TV. "Pura," he said in a firm tone, "do not try to dissuade our guest—I will watch out for Eduardo tomorrow. This is a matter to be settled entre hombres, between men." Turning your way, he said, "Let us adjourn to the *Toricuarto*."

"Then I will say goodnight," Pura responded with playful anger. "Once Fernando enters that room, he doesn't emerge for hours." She offered us two cheeks for kisses and retired with her graceful step. Now that she was gone, your fate was sealed for the next day.

We walked down a long, dark hall that became the labyrinth of the Cretan minotaur in your imagination spiked with sherry, Rioja and anisette. Fernando wavered ahead of you.

"Will we ever find our way out of the maze?" you asked.

"Your Ariadne has gone but do not worry. I will deliver you from the monster."

He stopped, stood at the threshold of a room, flicked a light-switch and pointed inside. *"Voilà."* You stepped forward. On the far wall a colossal head of the minotaur dominated the room: glassy eyes and thick, bossed, upturned horns.

"Welcome to the Toricuarto," said Fernando with exaggerated solemnity. "What would you call it in English?"

Silently you ran through the options—Bullfight Room, Bull Room, Taurine Room. Nothing worked. "Untranslatable."

"Good."

The walls and the ceiling were covered with paintings, photographs, posters, sculptures and memorabilia: reproductions of cave-drawings with ancient bulls and bisons, taurine statues from Crete and Mallorca, bright-colored pairs of banderillas with their small steel barbs; *monteras,* black toreros' caps; the broad-brimmed beaver skin hats worn by the horse-mounted *picadores;* unfurled capes and muletas; oils and and watercolors of bullfights by Bayeu, Goya, Fortuny, Zuloaga, Romero de Torres, Vázquez Díaz, Picasso, a few of them originals; multi-colored women's fans made of ivory, sandalwood, tortoise shell or mother-of-pearl with scenes from the plaza de toros on their silk, rice paper, cotton or lace.

Although you had been in your friend's apartment several times, you had never been admitted so far in, all the way to the Toricuarto. The afternoon and evening had been a sort of hierarchic ritual. First you had entered Fernando's study, the mostly male world of science, books and art. Next we had gone to the living room for supper with the women—the public place of food and drink, TV, the telephone. Finally we had passed through the labyrinth into this bizarre chamber, the masculine domain of bull and bullfight, the inmost sanctum, holy of holies.

Fernando guided as you stared in wonder. Portraits of bullfighters composed a museum gallery: the founding father, Pedro Romero; the legendary figures of *Pepe-Illo,* Paquiro, Lagartijo, Frascuelo, *Guerrita;* the creators of the modern art, Joselito and Belmonte; the Mexicans Rodolfo Gaona and Silverio Pérez, the Spaniards Marcial

Lalanda, Nicanor Villalta, Ignacio Sánchez Mejías who died "at exactly five o'clock in the afternoon"; the young, sanguine Joselito, jut-jawed Belmonte, the dour, long-faced Manolete. Enormous, yellowing, floor-to-ceiling posters with oil paintings by Ruano Llopis, Navarrete and Roberto Domingo announced corridas in Madrid, Sevilla, Valencia, Alicante, Murcia, Pamplona, Bilbao.

Fernando pointed proudly to a place of honor on the wall opposite the bull's head, where a glass niche contained a ticket from the plaza of Talavera de la Reina, dated 16 May 1920 and another from Linares, dated 28 August 1947—the two most infamous days in the history of toreo, when the exalted Joselito, followed by the revered Manolete had been gored to death. The Toricuarto resembled a shrine with the bull as godhead, Joselito and Manolete as his prophets, other matadores as the community of saints and Fernando as high priest. The whole room was a monument to the pagan, Celtiberian, Hispano-Arabic, Roman Catholic, Baroque, Goyesque, Romantic, gypsy, Andalusian, Castilian, Spanish American, folkloric, picturesque, tragic apotheosis of life, death and tauromaquia.

Fernando struck a match, lit votive candles beneath the stuffed head at one end of the Toricuarto and under the glass niche at the other. Turning off the light, he confided, "Electricity is a profanation here. The corrida requires the natural light of an arena or the candlelight of a chapel. Sun and shadow, *vida y muerte.*"

"Don't get so gloomy, Fernando. You might end up without a partner in the ring tomorrow."

"Let us forget that for now. At this moment the situation demands a nightcap. Let it be a royal drink," he said, opening a built-in cabinet on one wall, "since we are both named after monarchs, British or Spanish—Edward and Fernando."

"Some of the worst kings in both countries had our names."

"All were not bad. Some were even saints." Smiling, you thought Fernando could be the most religious of your friends in Spain. He also may have been one of the few devout, Catholic psychopathologists in his country or anywhere, undeniably the only one who fought bulls. In the wide world there was nobody else like Fernando, no other room like the Toricuarto.

Your host pointed to a row of bottles on the cabinet's lower shelf: domestic brandies like Duque de Alba, Cardenal Mendoza and Carlos I; anisettes, Bénédictine, green and yellow Chartreuse, vintage Ports. On the top shelf were ranked various liqueur glasses of fine crystal.

"That Port looks good," you said, pointing to a dark bottle of Taylor Fladgate.

"It is a 1948, almost as old as you. We were still mourning the death of Manolete that year. This wine may be a little heavy for the season but it is a superb vintage and there should be enough for two glasses. I hope there are not too many dregs in the bottom."

"I'll try it." All at once it seemed colder in that room without windows, surrounded by thick walls, deep in the interior of Fernando's house.

"Then I will join you, Eduardo. A propósito it is always cool in the Toricuarto because it is so distant from the street."

Cold as a tomb, you said to yourself, shivering. Once more Fernando had divined or at least coincided with your thoughts. You chose one of two leather armchairs, the only furniture besides the wooden cabinet.

Fernando handed you a glass of Port, ruby at the bottom, a rusty tint around the edges of crystal. He sat in the other chair and held up his drink, offering, "Salud! To your health! *Y que haya suerte,*" he added, the customary phrase for wishing a torero good luck before a bullfight.

"Thanks."

"Did you find a third man for tomorrow?"

"Yes."

"Who is he?"

"Alberto Flores, an aficionado who runs a bar downtown." He and Fernando belonged to opposite spheres of Madrid, you thought.

One dwelled in the old, seedy center of town while the other lived on a broad, tree-lined avenue.

Your host steepled his fingers and frowned. "Has this Alberto ever faced a bull with brave blood?"

"He's from the province of Sevilla."

"That virtually answers the question."

As we sipped our Port, the tapers' light danced on the walls. The drink warmed you inside, but your ears, nose, hands and feet felt even colder.

"Look, Eduardo," he said softly, "I know you are worried. Believe me when I say this—I would not insist unless it were for your own good. Remember that I am about a decade older than you, a doctor by profession and your bullfight counselor."

"You're a psychopathologist but to the best of my knowledge I don't suffer from a mental illness. I've run the encierro in Pamplona—it's been good for me at this stage of life. I don't feel the need to prove myself with a bull in the arena."

"*Un momento,*" Fernando said as he rose to relight one of the votive candles whose wax had burned down. He took his seat again. "Eduardo, without running the bulls you would not have lived the Sanfermines to the hilt. You would not be precisely the person you are today. Am I correct?"

"Yes. And I'm grateful that you urged me to run."

"The fiesta in Pamplona is a collective, democratic celebration. . ."

"That's what I like about it," you interrupted before Fernando could pursue his argument. "Feeling immersed in a crowd."

"On the other hand facing a brave bull in the ring is an individual, aristocratic rite. It is man confronting animal, intelligence against force, skill versus power, the soul vis-à-vis the flesh."

"When the rockets explode for the encierro, every man's also alone." That memory was still so fresh that the hair stood up on your arms.

"Believe me, my friend, not nearly as alone as a torero in the plaza—alone with a great burden of responsibility to himself and the public. Al buen entendedor, pocas palabras," Fernando ended with the familiar expression. "You mentioned skill in toreo. Hombre, I don't have it. It's not something anyone can acquire overnight." You took a compulsive swallow of the smooth, rich Port, whose aftertaste lingered.

"Especially if you go on drinking like that, Eduardo. This wine is for sipping, not gulping."

"If this were the last wine I ever drink, it would be a good finale."

"Now you are the one who sounds morbid."

"It's hard to avoid thoughts of mortality in a room decorated with the embalmed head of a fighting bull and shrines to dead toreros."

Fernando smiled. "I realize how much you love Spain, Eduardo, this country of ours that God or destiny shaped like a *piel de toro*, a bull's hide." As if the room represented the whole nation, he made a wide gesture with one arm. "If you want to grasp it you need to know the corrida. Remember what the regent María Cristina told her son, the future King Alfonso XIII—'One must go to the plaza de toros to understand the Spanish people.'"

"That didn't keep him from being tossed out of the country by the Republic."

"Among true aficionados the corrida transcends politics, Eduardo."

"I go to the bullfights whenever I'm in Spain, as I used to go in Mexico. That's enough for me." You sipped the Port. "Take Hemingway. He ran the encierro but never faced a bull or a brave calf in the ring."

"*Peor para él,*" So much the worse him.

"If running the encierro was good enough for Hem, it's enough for me."

"But I know you, my friend. You will never be satisfied with anything from the outside. After all you are partly Spanish yourself, right? Just as you had to run the bulls in order to understand the Sanfermines, you must face an animal with brave blood in order to comprehend toreo—to live it, to feel it from the inside. And be able to record it firsthand. I have invited you to the Toricuarto in honor of that occasion."

One of the votive candles flickered, sputtered, flickered again before dying in a ghost of black smoke. Its acrid odor hung in the air. You drank off the final drops of Port, bitter from the dregs.

Without speaking, Fernando walked to the cabinet, quenched the other candles. He led you out of the room, down the hall and through the penumbra to the front door. We embraced and said goodnight.

Falling asleep in the hotel room, you saw images of bulls, mazes and minotaurs. After lunch Alberto picked you up in his small Fiat coupe and drove us to the Paseo de la Castellana. We met Fernando on the sidewalk in front of his apartment building, where we climbed into his larger, newer car, a black Peugeot sedan. Alberto took the passenger's seat while you sat in the rear.

Fernando drove northwest toward the Sierra de Navacerrada. At first the conversation between the two men in front seemed strained. You could scarcely imagine a pair more different. One born a peasant, the other a patrician. One educated in the school of fields and streets, the other by the best universities in the world. One the owner of a bar, the other a doctor and writer.

We drove through the rolling Castilian landscape of scrub oaks, pines, granite outcroppings and stone walls. On both sides of the road we saw dark forms of fighting bulls with radiant hides and rippling muscles, grazing in the sun. Alberto broke the ice by launching into a popular song about a breeder in the south:

> Soy el mejó' ganaero
> der campo de Andalusía,
> Mi' toro' son lo' má' bravo' . . .

I'm the best rancher in Andalucía,
My bulls are the most brave ...

Fernando hummed along. Now he and Alberto would be companions for good, you thought, united by a passion for bulls and the corrida. The ten years of age that separated them, the light-years of class, birth and education, were obliterated by their afición and the song.

"There it is," Fernando announced. He indicated a group of long, low, whitewashed buildings, roofed with red tiles in the manner of a *cortijo* or ranch. Next to the corrals we saw a little bullring surrounded by a white wall, grandstands rising on the shady side.

"We are on time, *las cinco en punto*, five sharp," Fernando quoted, rubbing it in again.

As we descended from the car, we felt the dry summer air. You looked around: stark white bullring, steel-grey peaks of Navacerrada, starched blue sky. Castilla.

Dressed in a traje corto, a stocky, rough-skinned man greeted us. Fernando introduced us to Don Manuel, proprietor of Cortijo Bravo. The two began discussing the animals, gesticulating with their hands, whispering something they must have wanted nobody else to hear.

Alberto asked the owner where he could find a bathroom.

"First door on your left as you enter the building," Don Manuel said.

"*La meada del miedo,*" The piss of fear, Alberto joked, using the phrase for a torero's last visit to the urinal before a corrida.

While Fernando opened the trunk of his car, the owner inquired about your experience with fighting bulls.

"I've only run the encierro in Pamplona."

"Menos mal," Not all bad, he said.

Your friend removed a leather valise engraved with gold letters, "F.C.L." for his full, resonant name, Fernando Claramunt López.

Thinking how much your life had changed in twenty years or so, you recalled the initials on Gustavo's handmade boots.

Don Manuel led us inside, where equipment hung on the stucco walls: furled *capotes* and muletas, banderillas, red-hilted swords. Alberto joined us and took down one of the large capes, held it by the collar and placed it upright on the cement floor.

"See how it stand all by self" he asked or said. "That mean good capote. Now you try, Eduardo."

"Very different from our tennis gear," you told him, attempting a laugh. We crossed glances. Seeing the apprehension in your eyes, Alberto winced. Meanwhile Fernando had left with the other man.

You unhooked another capote from the wall. It felt much heavier than it appeared, faded magenta on the outside with a thick lining on the inside, pale yellow, to give it form and heft. You grasped the cape by the collar to stand it straight up. When you released it, the cloth sagged to the floor in a heap.

"Put that piece shit back, take mine," Alberto said, nudging your ribs and trying to hearten you.

With a new cape from the wall he cited an imaginary bull as he huffed *Ehe toro! Hu hu toro!"* He practiced a series of verónicas, making the capote's hem swish over the dirt floor.

Feeling awkward, you tried two or three passes with Alberto's first cape. Then you followed your friend, switching the capote for a muleta, the smaller cloth of red flannel, supported down the middle by a tapered wooden stick, used in the last stage of the bullfight.

Fernando emerged into the room, dressed in a traje corto, similar to Don Manuel's but better tailored and of higher quality. He wore grey, pocketless striped trousers with flared cuffs adorned by silver buttons; a short black jacket tapering sharply to a high, narrow waistline; an immaculate white shirt with an open, square-cut collar, silver studs and matching cufflinks; tan leather boots and a *sombrero cordobés*, the typical wide-brimmed, flat-topped hat of southern Spain, raked to one side.

Alberto whistled his admiration. He too wore *botas camperas,* the handmade, country-style boots sported by Fernando. Your shoes were the same you had worn to play tennis in Madrid and run the encierro in Pamplona; they looked fragile and all wrong for this place. Like you Alberto was dressed in a short-sleeved shirt and dark cotton pants.

"What are we going to face in the ring, maestro?" he asked the owner of Cortijo Bravo.

"A novillo, a two-year old bull," the man replied.

After smiling at those words, Fernando addressed you and Alberto. "Maybe I can also persuade Don Manuel to release one of his brave cows."

You could persuade him or anybody else, you told Fernando in silence.

"*Ya veremos,*" We'll see, the owner answered.

Fernando chose a cape and muleta and rehearsed a variety of fluid passes with each. When he had finished, Don Manuel escorted us to the bullring. The stands had been empty when we arrived. About a dozen people sat there now while others milled around the glaring white wall.

"Who are they?" you asked Fernando in English, the mother tongue making you more secure.

"Hangers-on," he answered in Spanish, the correct language for here, he understood. "Bullfighting has even more parasites than boxing."

A good comparison, you thought. Two rings—one square, one round—where you meet the Other, man or bull. You remembered boxing at the YMCA as a teenager: the anxiety before a match, the mystery of your opponent, the solitude as you entered that lurid space. In a foreign country years later, with people who were mostly strangers, speaking a language you knew but not your own, you felt even lonelier, more afraid.

The three of us took our spots behind a *burladero,* one of the planked shelters or barriers placed at intervals just inside the wooden wall around the arena, large enough for a man to pass through but too narrow for a horned creature. We stood opposite the gate where the bull would enter from the corrals. Without anyone stating it, we all assumed Fernando would be *director de lidia,* the torero who supervised the fight. He decided Alberto should go first, followed by you and himself; each of us would make a few passes with the capote in that order, then in turn with the muleta. By the time it met Fernando, the animal would be wiser and more dangerous, having learned from our mistakes.

Don Manuel swung open the *toril,* the broad gate from the corrals to the ring. Within seconds a black, wide-horned young bull ran onto the golden sand, skidded on his front hooves and halted in the sun to scan the arena, head erect, ears twitching.

"*Está bien,*" Fernando uttered with reverence.

"*Qué bonito!*" Alberto murmured.

The creature's power and beauty made your heart leap. It was as if the emotion of the encierro were focused in one instant onto that small ring, that circle of sand, like sunshine through a lens.

Alberto stepped cautiously from the burladero with his cape. He took his position by the wall. As soon as the bull spotted the man, it charged. Alberto stood straight, spread the capote and made three passes, leading the animal toward the center of the arena.

"Our friend knows what he is doing," Fernando said without removing his eyes for a second from either Alberto or the bull. "Notice how he stays in *tablas*—at the edge of the ring—so the novillo follows its natural tendency to hook away from the wall and the torero."

Our friend did more passes, taking the bull to the opposite side of the plaza. "He yours now Eduardo!" Alberto yelled, breathing hard, taking refuge behind another barrier. His broken English jarred, so wildly out of place here.

Fernando gripped your forearm. (You recalled when Rich had squeezed it in Valencia, Gustavo in Orizaba before that.) "Be sure not to stray from tablas, Eduardo," he pronounced with a grave tone in Spanish. "And whatever you do, never, *jamás* let the novillo pass between you and the wall. We will be ready to *hacer el quite*, to help if you need us."

Standing next to Fernando, watching Alberto with the cape, you had been secure. Now you were entirely alone and uncertain as you slipped through the burladero and stepped into the arena. Nobody can help when you face a bull or run the encierro, you thought. In fact you remembered Pamplona, the way one feels alert, all the senses alive, taking in every detail of light and shade, each smell and sound, but at the same time moving as in a dream.

When the bull detected your movement, he made a three-quarters spin and stood on the line that divided the sand between sun and shadow, panting, a wisp of mucus from his nostrils blowing in the breeze from the sierra. Before you could set yourself, he dropped his head and pushed off, kicking up the dirt while you lowered the cape, heard him snort as he passed through the cloth, then turned fast to assault again. It happened quickly, much quicker than the encierro: you did not have time to feel the dread tight in your stomach, nor to heed Fernando's advice, forgetting it and the crowd, the mountains and sky, everything but the animal who was already coming again, going for your body instead of the cape that seemed much smaller each second, all that separated you from the beast who was tightening the circle of his charges until you had no space to maneuver and Fernando was there miraculously, drawing the bull away with his capote. You took cover behind the shelter with Alberto, who clapped you on the shoulder, laughing. "This no tennis match, right Eduardo?"

Fernando stood with his back to the wall, his feet together. He executed a clean verónica, another, a third, moving the novillo toward the center of the ring, and finished with a half-verónica, shortening the swing of the cloth, turning the animal so hard that it stopped short while your friend gathered the folds of his cape against his right hip. Fernando looked disdainfully over his shoulder at the bull first, next at the sky before striding away as the crowd applauded.

"Your amigo he torero," Alberto said in macaronic English or Spanish.

Fernando joined us and determined we should let the novillo rest before the final stage. "He is a beautiful *torito*. We want to keep him fresh." After a minute or so he announced, *"Ahora sí,* let the last tercio begin."

As you stood behind the barrier with Alberto, you felt less frightened than before, in spite of the close escape a few minutes ago. Anticipation can be worse than the thing itself, more nightmarish, you thought, in both the encierro and the bullfight.

Alberto strode forward and cited with a muleta in his left hand, a sword in his right. The novillo attacked, the man was caught off balance, tripped, recovered, received the animal on his left, almost pinned against the wall. He extricated himself with several right-handed passes, each one a little further from the side of the ring, holding the cloth extended by the sword, talking to the bull, *"Sí, toro, sí."* Alberto ended with the customary *pase de pecho* across his chest, grinning up at the crowd. His shirt, pants, face and arms were coated with dust.

He did another set with the muleta, broken by more falls. Keeping his gaze fixed on the arena, Fernando commented, "I do not know who is more of a bull, Alberto or the novillo. He is built like a four-year-old Miura or Victorino and he fights in the rough-and-tumble style of El Cordobés. Actually his body reminds me of a rugby player more than a torero. But he has *duende*, spirit to spare."

Alberto left the animal out of breath near the wall by the planked burladero. Instructing our robust friend to stand between us and the novillo, Fernando took your arm and led you onto the sand. We were about to celebrate our own, unofficial, mock-heroic version of the *alternativa*, the ceremony in which a senior bullfighter sponsors a younger torero upon whom he confers the rank of *matador de toros*, while a third man serves as witness.

Declaiming the statutory words, Fernando handed you his muleta and sword. You recalled how José Mari had given you his red scarf of San Fermín. Again you felt moved, but this time the trep-idation and your friend's ironic look prevented you from crying. Following the next part of the rite, as you had observed it in Mexico and Spain, you passed your cape to Fernando. "Que haya suerte, matador," he said in earnest but with a know-ing half-smile. We gave each other the traditional embrace to close the ritual. Alberto, as designated witness, walked over to shake your hand.

Both men returned to the barrier while you approached the bull. He did not move at once. You had the chance to see him close as he stared at you sideways with dark-lashed eyes: his pointed, ivory horns, beginning to curve forward like those of a mature *toro de lidia;* a tuft of hair on his forehead, his long head tapering to a russet snout, flared nostrils dripping snot, sweat-shiny front and flanks, hanging dewlap, testicles and hairy penis, front legs placed slightly to the left, rear legs separated and poised to release. During those seconds while the novillo rested, you fathomed why Fernando wanted you to con-front a brave-blooded animal in the arena, the one place in the world where you can participate in a formal spectacle with a creature intent on killing you.

You held the scarlet flannel so that its surface tautened, made larger by the length of sword in your right hand. They too seemed weightier than they appeared. Could you manipulate them with suf-ficient speed, you wondered, as you had worried your legs might not carry you fast enough in Pamplona. No running here: this was not a race or sport but a solitary encounter between you and a novillo. He was watching you keenly, turning his body your way, squaring his front legs.

Shaking the cloth, you cited him close to the wall. He twitched an ear, raised the crest of muscle on his neck, lifted his tail and charged, lowering his head into the muleta as he went by, air hissing from his nostrils. You did an about-face to receive him in the opposite direc-tion with the same hand, stepping farther from the wooden wall. He stormed again, once more, again and you could not believe that he was going for the flannel instead of your body. Recalling how Alberto had terminated his series, you passed the bull to the left across your chest, lifting the cloth in order to raise his head and bring him to a halt.

You glanced away for a second and suddenly Fernando and Alberto were calling from the shelter, *"Eduardo! Cuidado que viene!"*—voices from a dream—and the novillo had rushed before you could take position by the wall, he hooked into your legs and butted, knocking you to the ground where you scrambled to your feet for a new assault, he bumped you in the shins, turning faster this time as you felt the exhilaration and terror of struggling for your life, lost to everything but the animal, remembering in flashes the encierro in Pamplona, the night in Orizaba, those moments when you had to call on instincts to survive, when you felt wholly fearful and present, now more than ever, falling and getting up again, dust in eyes, nose and mouth, legs aching from blows of horns and hooves, thinking you would never escape, stumbling and falling, prone on the sand with your back to the bull, blindly, everlastingly waiting for the next smash when Fernando's familiar boots appeared just inches from your face, the bottom of his cape brushing the ground as he drew the novillo smoothly away, talking to him, *"Ven toro, torito,"* saving you like a referee who calls a technical knockout, and your other friend lifted you by the armpits, dragging you out of the ring and behind the wall.

"You all right?" Alberto asked.

You could only breathe in and out for a reply.

"Watch this," he said in a hush, with a jut of his chin pointing toward Fernando. Our older friend had the muleta in his left hand and was doing a linked, unhurried set of *natural* passes, making them look so simple when you knew, so much better than before, that they required a discipline of years, not to mention talent and courage.

"He make love to bull," Alberto said.

As we regarded Fernando in action, you felt an even greater respect for him and the animal. That creature descended from beings who had roamed the primeval forests of the continent where we stood—a continent whose very name stemmed from the story of a bull, the Rape of Europa—a wild race of gods worshipped throughout the Mediterranean world, now reduced to Spain, Portugal and a handful of countries in Spanish America. That was what Fernando wanted you to understand, to feel, you suspected vaguely as we watched: the deep layers beneath this rite and the half-serious formality of the alternativa.

He performed a complete faena except for the kill, offering us a lesson in valor, skill and grace. When he had tired the novillo, he opened the corral himself, led the bull inside, closed the gate with a flourish. The public, somehow grown larger, gave him a long ovation.

Fernando neared the burladero. Catching his breath, he said, "Now you know what it is like to be *cara a cara*, face to face with a god and your own death, Eduardo. And life—*esta vida breve*, This brief life of ours."

Without delay he asked or directed Don Manuel to release a three-year-old *vaquilla* or brave cow. Nobody could refuse Fernando. As we waited, he turned to you and said, "Most spectators ignore the female side of fighting stock, the cows who give birth to the bulls. Eduardo, I believe the animals' bravery comes through the mothers' blood while their *estampa*—their size and form—come through the father."

The creature burst into the ring, much larger than the novillo, with a pair of horns almost the size of a full-grown fighting bull's. Alberto and you both realized that we were outclassed. We stood behind the shelter, watching Fernando cite the animal with his capote. Knowing how dangerous the cow could be, Don Manuel took a place behind another barrier himself, cape at the ready.

After testing the vaquilla, Fernando did a series of slow passes, ending with another perfect *media verónica*. He could not continue because the cow, unlike the younger bull, would have required punishment from a picador's lance in order to bring her head down, low enough to work her with the muleta. Don Manuel opened the gate, and Fernando enticed her into the corral.

No matter where you are in Spain, even at a small bullring in the foothills of the Navacerrada Mountains, there's a drink nearby. Don Manuel, the proprietor in person, served us the conventional chatos, the little glasses of red wine, at the makeshift bar inside the building, only a few yards from the arena.

As the three Spaniards talked, you remained silent, distressed by your clumsy show. Fernando came in once again for the *quite*. "Eduardo," he said for all to hear, "you made up in *vergüenza torera* and grit what you lacked in elegance today."

"*Sí señó*," Alberto concurred.

"*Pa' gringo*," At least for a gringo, Don Manuel added.

"Do you understand the term?" Fernando asked in order to deflect the man's words, which had not made you feel better.

"More or less but tell me anyway."

"Vergüenza torera refers to a bullfighter's professional pride."

"I wouldn't say I'm a professional." We laughed, even the gruff Don Manuel, with the bonhomie of men who've been together in a bullring.

"We could also describe it as *pundonor*, a personal sense of honor," Fernando added, looking straight into your eyes. He placed his sword hand, the right, on your left shoulder, leaving it there for a half-minute or so. When he dropped his arm, most of your humiliation fell away too.

After the first round of drinks Fernando excused himself to change clothes. "It would not be correct to go home like this, dressed in a traje corto," he told us. "*Hay que hacer como Dios manda*, We must do as God commands. And by the way, remember—God's a Spaniard and an aficionado."

Soon we mounted in the car. As we moved along the road, you recalled the late summer afternoons, long ago, when John would drive us home to Los Angeles after weekends of bullfights and whoring in Tijuana. There had been another kind of sex at Cortijo Bravo.

210

If Fernando had made love to the animals, one of them had ravished you. Your body felt broken and abused: bumps, scratches and horn-burns covered your arms, legs, ribs and buttocks. Your left tennis shoe was falling apart at the heel, where the bull must have stomped it with a hoof. In spite of your failure in the ring you did not feel ashamed, because your two companions were treating you like the member of a brotherhood who had completed a rite of passage.

We were all seated in the front of the car now: Fernando, the doctor and writer, at the wheel; Alberto, the former peasant, on the passenger's side; you, the middle-class American, between them. Just as John and you had hardly spoken on the road back from Tijuana, the three of us said few words on the return to Madrid. What could we say that would not demean our experience? Through the windows we saw the silhouettes of great, hump-necked, close-horned fighting bulls grazing in the fields.

15. Marga

She was living that fall in the foothills of the mountains between the old kingdoms of León and Asturias. Since she did not have a telephone, you surprised her when you arrived on a cool, bright afternoon. Marga was feeding the pigeons in a ramshackle dovecot behind the stone house.

"Eduardo! I thought you might show up."

"Why?"

"I dreamed about you the other night."

"I always said you were a seer."

"No, just a good witch." Marga laughed, squinting her blue-grey eyes. They seemed to have aged since you had seen her a few months ago. They were the far-seeing eyes of someone who has lived for a long time in open, solitary places. We embraced.

"I know what you're thinking," she said with a tone of feigned guilt. "Sorry to look like this." Although she was the freest woman you had met in Spain, Marga preserved a kind of casual decorum in the company of men.

You did not attempt to make a gallant denial. Instead you thought that most women would be glad to look like Marga as she stood there in overalls and high, mud-spattered boots: clear eyes, arched brows, salient cheekbones, small chin, all her features rounded by the auburn hair that fell to her shoulders. She appeared fragile yet undaunted, gamely open to life. As your friend Rodrigo said of certain women, *"Sabe estar"*: she simply knows how to be there, or here, anywhere.

"Look at these birds," she said, pointing to the dovecot. They were jostling at the front of the wire-mesh cage, poised to lunge on the seeds that Marga held in her hands. "Doves are supposed to be symbols of peace but they're as violent among themselves as men or women. I have to feed the youngest by hand so the older ones won't take their food."

She opened the lopsided door and walked to the rear of the cage. There she fed, grain by grain, a little dove who was cowering on the dirt floor. The fat-chested birds in front cooed and flapped their wings in predatory arousal. Caressing its downy, iridescent neck, Marga lifted the baby dove for you to see.

She placed a finger on the band around the bird's throat. "The Arab poets in Andalusia called this ringlet *el collar de la paloma,* the dove's necklace. They compared it to a rainbow or mother-of-pearl." You pictured Khedidja, her gold anklet, the ring around her toe. Marga handed you the small bird, whose warmth sank into your palms.

She returned the dove to the rear of the cage and closed the dovecot behind her. "Eduardo, you're quieter than usual."

"Remembering."

"You still haven't gotten over the divorce?"

"It wasn't that. Or maybe I remembered something because I haven't gotten over the divorce—I don't know."

"Mine's not going well. Which is worse, a bad marriage or a bad divorce? The main thing is to accept your pain, live through it and face the future with a fresh heart." Her eyes turned toward the mountains. You admired Marga's sad courage, the way she's learned to live with hope in spite of losses.

"*Venga,* I'll show you some more animals," she said, returning from her memories too. "They're so much better than people."

"Then I'll leave you alone with them." In jest you spun on your heels.

With both hands she caught you by the waist. "Some people— not everyone, *tonto.*"

As you followed Marga to the far side of the house, her hair shone in the October light. Other times she had worn it blond or

214

red, short as a boy's or long as a horse's mane, tumbling to the small of her back. Marga was your first Spanish friend who belonged to a younger generation: a sure sign of your age. Her élan, her wisdom, her melancholy erased the ten years between us.

A sparse flock of sheep was grazing beyond a crumpled wall, tended by three Basque sheepdogs. Two of these had rough, yellowish coats while the third had smooth, cinnamon-colored hair. As we drew closer to them, the sun felt good on your face and neck.

The dogs surrounded Marga. A ewe and a lamb also snuggled at her legs. Both had a grey body with a black face, ears and belly. Marga talked to them, petted their fleecy necks, gave them something from the pockets of her overalls.

"These are the true animals of peace," she said.

"Are they merinos?"

She smiled. "Just because that's my family name doesn't mean I can afford merino sheep with their heavy fleece. No, these belong to a common breed who barely have enough wool to keep them warm during the long winters here. Next to them a merino is like a toro bravo compared to a domestic bull." How far away Fernando and the mostly male world of the corrida seemed now.

Marga continued playing with the ewe and lamb, touching, talking, whispering to them. You recalled Khedidja surrounded by the stray dogs and cats of Barcelona. Perhaps what you told Marga is right: the breakup of your marriage leads you to recall better days, those of that first trip to Spain. At the same time you missed your son terribly, with an ache in the ribs. He made you think of Marga's daughter, slightly younger, who would also be a child of divorce.

"How's the rest of your family?" you asked.

Absorbed in her animals, Marga had almost forgotten you. "Sorry, Eduardo," she said, turning to look at you with her wistful eyes. "What?"

"I was wondering about your daughter."

"She's a survivor like you and me, like your son. I believe some children come out of divorce stronger, free of the illusions that made us so vulnerable." A movement caught Marga's attention. "That's my favorite," she said, gazing at a chestnut filly gamboling in a corral beyond the sheepfold. "Without my *criaturas* I couldn't have survived among human beings."

With the sunlight slanting into our eyes, we started walking to the stone house. "They've taught me so much," Marga resumed. "The perfection of their silence, *sabes?*" She paused. "When I was a girl growing up in the Franco years I had ducks, cats, fish, larks. I felt closer to my pets than to people, above all those in power—politicians, priests, nuns, teachers and even parents. Those men and women preached at us, making us deny our bodies, our needs, our sexuality. Just by their presence my animals let me stay in touch with myself, with real life and the world."

As she spoke, you could not help comparing Marga, who loved those small, humble creatures, to Fernando, who worshiped the most dangerous of beasts, the Iberian fighting bull.

"We've never talked about the corrida," you told her.

"It's one of the few things under the stars we haven't discussed." Marga's laugh sounded like fast water in a brook.

"Pues what do you think about it?"

"Hombre, I have nothing against toreo when it's done honestly, with full respect for both the animals and the men—or women, because there are a few *matadoras* now. The fighting bull is a magnificent being, a god with four legs." Marga frowned. "What I oppose are abuses like the horn-shaving or the brutal fiestas and capeas in towns and villages where my prehistoric compatriots—all men, naturally—take out their resentment on novillos, calves or brave cows, assaulting them with rocks, sticks, knives and whatever else they find. Not to mention other 'traditions'"—she made quotation marks with her fingers—"like throwing a live goat from a bell tower, killing a donkey with clubs or ripping off a goose's head as a proof of manhood. In the 1950s and 60s I witnessed these horrors in my own province of León. You can imagine how they affected a little girl who loved animals." Marga inhaled deeply to stifle her rage. "I think it would be better to perform these acts on the people who practice and support them. That would allow them to experience an even greater emotion, no? You see I'm a terrorist, Eduardo. Not one who wounds or kills but one who shocks people in order to change them."

We were approaching the front of Marga's house. "The Church says animals don't have souls," you said, "so it's alright for us to kill them."

She sighed. "Their argument no longer holds water, Eduardo. For me that filly over there, my three dogs, my sheep and doves—each one of them has more of a soul than the men who commit the barbarities I've described to you. A lot of people would agree with me nowadays, even some Spaniards." She paused. "What about you?"

"I'm one of those who would agree. Yet toreo can be so beautiful that I couldn't approve its abolition—that would be a loss forever." We had reached the house, where we stopped on the stone doorstep. "If the corrida were banned, brave bulls would eventually cease to be raised, just as thoroughbred horses would decline without the sport of racing. Hundreds, maybe a thousand years of bloodlines would disappear. Also I'm unconvinced by persons who campaign for animal rights and treat their pets more humanely than they treat other people."

"*Ya*," Marga responded, scanning the sky. "We still have several hours of daylight, Eduardo. Why don't we go hunt for *setas*, wild mushrooms? They're in season and we could cook them for supper. You're staying, right?"

"The last bus from the village left more than an hour ago. I'll spend the night as long as you don't poison me."

"Remember—I'm a good witch." She smiled and narrowed her eyes. "I'll show you how to tell the safe mushrooms from the bad ones." Marga opened the unlocked door of heavy oak and dissolved into the darkness of her house.

In less than fifteen minutes she had prepared a picnic basket, and we were climbing toward the sierra. The Montes de León rose above us, jagged, grey and snow-peaked. Swaying her elbows and singing

an old Leonese ballad from these mountains, Marga strode ahead
with the straw basket on one arm:

> Mañanita, mañanita,
> mañanita de San Simón,
> estaba una señorita
> sentada en su balcón . . .

"*Hay que ensanchar el tórax!* Open up your windpipe and let in
the clean air, Eduardo!" she shouted after the final verses. "Singing,
hiking, mountains, animals—they'll cure us!"

Then she chose some tunes for us to sing: an Aragonese jota, student songs from Salamanca and Santiago de Compostela, "*Quel maz-
zolin di fiori*" from the Italian Alps, even "My Darling Clementine." It
felt good to be out of the city and in the sierra with Marga. We were
about a thousand meters up, where the white peak of Mampodre
rose ahead of us, more than twice as high. The heady air almost stung
as you breathed in.

Climbing and singing, we reached a stream that flowed down
the side of the mountain. Trees lined its banks: some evergreens—
spruces and pines—others like poplars, beech and birches whose
yellow leaves glanced in the sunlight.

Marga set the basket on the shore, opened it and slipped out two
dark-green bottles. "I also brought a hunk of sheep's cheese and a loaf
of bread from the village," she said over the sound of rushing water.
She had been hiking so briskly that nobody would have guessed her
basket held that abundance. "And these of course," she added, smiling and holding up two chatos for drinking the wine. "I'm going to
cool the bottles." She moved nimbly to the water's edge.

You followed, still breathing hard from the climb, feet squelching
in the wet grass. When you caught up with Marga, she was seated on
the bank where the stream dropped in a short fall, sending up a spray
and making a small rainbow. She had removed her boots and was
dangling her feet in the current. Above us a great white oak extended

its branches with blood-red and golden leaves, its roots emerging from the shore, its trunk wet with vapor, the upper foliage flashing with bright-winged birds who flew around it, in and out, fishing for insects on the water.

"This is my tree and my stream," Marga said, lying on her back. She extended both arms toward the sky. "In a spot like this I know why the ancients believed rivers, woods and trees had spirits. I feel more at home here than in any house I've ever lived in, especially in the cities, Eduardo. This is where I come to bathe, to look, to think, to be."

"What a place, what a tree, Marga! I can see you here as a wood nymph—a dryad or water sprite."

"I am," she answered with a playful smile. She sat up, kneeled, put her hands in the stream and pulled a load of round, shiny stones from the bottom. With them she made a little dam for the bottles. When they were snugly in place, like two infants in a cradle, she cupped her hands to wash her face in the stream.

Marga leaned over the edge and submerged her head, her long hair buoyed by the current and trailing downstream. She lifted her face from the water, sputtering, "Try it, Eduardo!"

You knelt over the stream. Before you could lower your face to the surface, Marga splashed you with the icy water, giggling as she jumped to her feet. "Look!" she cried and pointed to a clump of small green leaves, "*Berros!* What do you call them in English?"

"Watercress."

"Let's taste it."

After plunging onto the moist turf, she snapped off two bunches, gave you one and nibbled on the other. You chewed the cold, crisp, peppery-tasting stalks and leaves. You've entered Marga's sphere, you thought, on the shore of a stream by a waterfall, in the shade of a sprawling tree, your face soaked with water, eating a wild herb.

Before you could settle into that world, she sprang to her feet. "Let's go look for *setas* while there's still good light." She romped to the picnic basket, pulled out a cloth sack, wheeled and was off without waiting for you.

For the next hour or so—time has another dimension in Marga's realm—we hunted for mushrooms on the banks of the stream and in shady woods, breathing the thin smells of autumn. You recall her dancing in and out of dappled light, singing more ballads and folksongs, talking to you or herself or maybe the trees, crying out when she found a cluster of setas like jewels in the damp earth, showing you the prized *oronjas* or *níscalos* and the toxic, evil-looking *matamoscas* and *cicutas verdes*. Then she was frisking back to the stream to slosh in her bare feet, embracing, kissing and climbing her tree, playing Peter Pan on the lookout for Captain Hook, a Moorish girl watching for her lover from a tower of the Alhambra, an Indian brave scouting for cavalry, Marga shimmying down the trunk and taking our treasure to the site where we'd left the basket, falling on her back in the turf, legs and arms spread-eagle, looking up at the sky.

We packed the cooled wine and fresh mushrooms and started down the hill. She found a spot for our picnic, a clearing by a crumbling wall covered with ivy, overlooking the valley and a village below. The sun had dropped in the deep-sea blue sky, where a few clouds had turned pink and red. While Marga laid out a tablecloth and the food, you opened the first bottle with a corkscrew, poured the red wine into the chatos. We squatted on the ground.

"Salud!" she cried.

"Salud! Thanks for today, Marga. I needed it."

"I need it every day."

The bread, cheese and wine tasted luscious in the open air, better than the most refined cuisine. As we ate and drank, Marga removed the setas from the cloth sack—various kinds, some small as a thimble, others large as a fist, their colors from creamy white to greys, browns and tender orange.

"Wait till we cook them! They're so rich that you can serve them as a main course without meat or fish—even in Spain."

"Why do Spaniards have such a passion for wild mushrooms? Every fall I hear about people who die from eating them."

"Those are foragers who don't know their species. When you taste what we've found today you'll understand why people take risks. *Claro,* our machistas say they're willing to do it because mushrooms are such potent aphrodisiacs."

"Is it true?"

"*Vaya,* I can't speak for men. All I know is that they make me feel good. Our word seta is also a vulgar term for the vagina." She pronounced these words with no sexual undertone or hint of embarrassment. With Marga it was possible to discuss anything without the innuendo that seeps into most friendships between men and women, especially in Latin America and Spain.

You picked up a mushroom, rubbed the dark membranes beneath its cap, raised it to your nose and breathed in the earthy odor. Once more you acknowledged the brilliance of the Castilian language and imagination.

"Marga, we have a word in English that you'll like. We call the poisonous or inedible species 'toadstools,' from their shape. Also because you'd probably find toads and mushrooms in the same habitat."

"Some Welsh or Irish poet must have coined that one. You're right, I love that word—"Toad-stool!" she cried with open vowels, making it sound more Spanish than English. "That reminds me of the frogs and toads I used to take home from trips to the countryside when I was a girl. Like most Spaniards in the cities we lived in an apartment building with no yard so I had to keep those animals in the bathtub. When my family protested I hid them in the most unlikely places where they'd get lost and appear in a few weeks or months—*pobrecitos,* poor things—dried up like leaves, like little mummies. I saved them in my pet cemetery beneath my bed until my mother threw them away. It took me years to forgive her for that."

We reclined against the wall and fell into silence, deep enough for memories and dreams. Marga's story brought to mind your childhood pets, dogs, chiefly the one who used to race with you on the beach in California. Then you remembered Barbara González running along the shore when she was just a girl, the first Hispanic woman you ever knew, as you sat by another now, Margarita Merino, all these years later. You felt enough confidence with her, free of erotic entanglements, to confess what you had never admitted to anyone.

As we drank our wine and watched the sun dropping to the horizon, you told her about Barbara on the sand long ago, about your Spanish great-great-grandmother, how you had tried to find your own Latin roots and history in Mexico first, afterwards in Spain, the travel, the friends, women, the rest. You had hardly known that girl on the beach, yet now it seemed that she had foretold your search from Upper to Lower California, the Pacific to the Gulf of Mexico, the Caribbean and the Atlantic, from New World to the Old, back there and here again. It had all made a sort of arc that ended in this spot, for now, with Marga in the sierra, both of us with ruined marriages and a child of divorce. She listened carefully but did not reply, as though she were pondering your words the way her sheep ruminated on the grass.

We sat watching the deepening violet sky. A small wind rose. You felt a soft tiredness spreading inside of you from the walk, the food and wine, the relief of unburdening yourself.

Still staring to the west, she spoke. "Eduardo, you've been lucky to live in two worlds—or between them. Do you recall the night we met?"

"Nobody could forget meeting you, Marga."

"I was in charge of the guest list and I didn't know you or your wife. None of the hosts could explain how two strangers managed to crash a private book-launch party. There were a lot of Spanish writers who would have loved to be there in your place."

"Someday I'll tell you the story."

"Anyhow you've seen us from the inside, Eduardo. You've written about it for people who never could have done that, mostly foreigners but Spaniards too. The fact that you've had a broken marriage doesn't mean your whole life has been wrong. If that were so mine would also be a mistake, not to mention the men and women we know and admire—think of all the friends, writers, artists, teachers!" Spreading her arms, she asked, "If our lives were failures could we take pleasure in a day like this? Would we feel as blessed as I do now to be with a friend, drinking wine, eating bread and cheese, watching the sunset on an autumn afternoon? No. There are many kinds of love and the deepest comes through loss." She turned her eyes from the setting sun and looked at you. "I can see your future clearly, Eduardo. And don't forget . . ."

"What?"

"I'm a good witch." Seeing your smile, she said, "Escucha. Don't renounce the road you've taken between two worlds—your road. In my dream the other night I saw you making a journey to the sea. You were alone but you were free, at peace with yourself. What else can we ask of life, *verdad*? Don't abandon your road, don't close yourself to love, don't forsake that little boy's quest on the beach in California."

Marga leaned her head on your shoulder. You felt her warmth against the cold air. The sun fell in the sky, shadows lengthened, the dark grew around us. When we stood to leave, an orange moon, almost full, rose behind us in the east. Its light showed the way home.

Marga. NORBERTO CABEZAS

16. Madrid

El **Callejón de la Ternera** is a passageway too narrow for a car.

El Callejón de la Ternera. MANUEL JIMÉNEZ

Long before it became the fashion, the restaurant had acquired its sonorous name from its street, Alley of the She-Calf. Although you knew it was too early for supper, you had taken the 9:30 invitation as seriously as a newcomer to Spain. Sunshine had chased the storm, light shone in the western sky above the buildings, and the asphalt was wet from rain.

Manolo Jiménez, the round-faced, olive-skinned owner of El Callejón, welcomed you. *"Buenas tardes, Eduardo. Es muy temprano todavía,"* It's way too early still. He drew a glass of Valdepeñas from a barrel in the tavern bar by the front door. "Muy temprano," Manolo repeated, handing you the wine, blood-red in the twilight.

You stepped into the main dining room with its walls of mahogany. They were covered with copper pans and kettles, ceramic vases, dried twigs of beech and thyme, autographed photos of bullfighters from the 1950s, 60s and 70s—Diego Puerta, El Viti, Antonio Ordóñez, Curro Romero. Around the solid oak tables the empty chairs had wooden frames and strips of tanned leather for seats. During forty years the feet of waiters and clients had smoothed and shaded the tile floor to the color of an old red wine. Lifting your glass, you tasted the Valdepeñas, light but a little acid on the tongue.

In a far corner you saw the room's only round table. Above it a bronze plaque read: *"Éste fue el rincón favorito del ilustre escritor y amigo Ernest Hemingway,"* This was the corner of the famous writer and friend . . . As always he had chosen a strategic place where his flanks were protected, where he commanded a view, where he could see better than he could be seen. Like a fighting bull in his querencia he was most formidable there, most himself.

You returned to the tavern bar where men had begun to gather, drinking beer, wine or pale sherry in tapered glasses. From there you stepped into the alley to mingle with the gathering crowd. It felt much cooler outside.

A minute later Fernando and Pura appeared. We embraced. You told them, "I'm relieved to see you." Addressing Pura, you said, "It's also nice to have a woman here."

She must have sensed my nerves. "Are you all right, Eduardo?"

"Bueno, better than the day we faced the bull at Cortijo Bravo. That reminds me—how was the corrida today, Fernando?"

"Rainy and so-so," he answered with a back-and-forth motion of his wrist. He sighted a waiter and signaled for two wines with the fingers of one hand.

226

Pura asked, "Is this the first time you've had a *presentación* for a book, Eduardo?"

"Yes."

More men arrived, accompanied by the odd woman or two. As we drank our wine and talked, we realized something had changed. Instead of milling between the alleyway and the bar, speaking in their usual resonant tones, the men had formed small groups and were making fierce gestures that seemed out of proportion to their hushed voices. Of the few women who were present, all but Pura had withdrawn to the restaurant's outside wall, from where they observed, mere witnesses to the male spectacle.

"Wait here," Fernando told us. When he left, you felt more anxious, almost the way you had felt without him at your side in the bullring last summer.

Pura knew. "Don't worry, Eduardo. They should be serving soon—it's about ten o'clock."

When Fernando returned, he told us with a confidential air: "There is a problem with one of the guests."

"Who?" Pura asked.

"Antonio D. Olano."

"Olano!" she pronounced under her breath. "No me digas. Do you know him, Eduardo?

"Not in person. I've skimmed one or two of his books and listened to his late-night radio show."

"Somehow he contrived to get an invitation," Fernando told us with a scowl, "but most of these journalists refuse to share a meal with him."

"Why?"

"Some are old-timers who wrote for the Republic during the Civil War. A couple of them even knew Ernesto. They allege this man is mainly here to publicize a book he is supposedly writing on Hemingway, who Olano believes was a fake and did not really understand the bullfight or Spain." Fernando whispered, "This character has been known to cause scandals before."

"He's also an alcoholic," Pura said.

"More to the point, he supported the Caudillo," Fernando added.

"The guy has everything against him," you tried to laugh. "I'm starting to feel sorry for him."

"If you knew Olano, you would not," Fernando uttered with the dead-serious intonation he had used to warn of danger at Cortijo Bravo. "But you should understand that these journalists are liberals who would oppose Olano in any case."

"Eduardo," Pura explained, "many of them suffered censorship, prison, torture or exile under Franco. That's why they can't abide him."

"I suppose that's also why Olano can't bear Hemingway," you said. "These Spaniards refuse to forget the Civil War."

"We cannot forget it," Fernando stated while he regarded the crowd, "nor should we." He paused. "As far as I can tell, *ABC* is the single major newspaper who has not sent a reporter tonight. They still associate Ernesto with the Republic—with Socialists, Reds and anarchists." Your friend enunciated the words with an inflection that showed his own distaste for those people.

"It sounds as if you're on Olano's side."

"No. But not because of his politics."

"Why then?"

Fernando formed an ironic smile on his lips. "Remember what Ernesto said—there is no such thing as writers of the right or left, just good or bad writers. Well he was a good one and this man is not."

We all laughed.

"Where is Olano?" you asked.

Fernando leaned into the doorway, scanning the interior. "Look beyond the tavern, Eduardo." You bent forward. "See the large man at the first table of the dining room, ranting at your publisher, a pair of journalists and the owner of El Callejón?"

"Not very well. I'm going inside. Perdón."

After walking through the bar and entering the dining room, you saw Manolo standing above a table where a Gargantuan, ruddy-faced man was seated, arguing with the others, waving his arms. His enormous person dominated the restaurant like a sumo wrestler in the ring or a fighting bull in the plaza. That table, that dining room might have been a primitive forest with male animals bellowing at each other, lowering their horns not for females but for the only things more important than sex in Spain: pride, dignity, respect. One can call them things because in this country they're as real as the red wine, as the cruets of olive oil and vinegar on the tables at El Callejón.

Spotting you, one of the journalists rose from Olano's table and approached.

"We're doing this for you, Señor Estánton," he said in the Spanish way, cupping his hands around your ear without ceasing to watch the sparring at the table. "If Olano stays we have no option but to leave. We refuse to break bread with a man like him. It's a question of pundonor, a point of honor—he stands for everything we've fought since the war. He's here to promote his book and sabotage yours."

"What difference does it make if he stays? Controversy can be healthy. Anyhow I'm capable of defending my book and Hemingway's reputation. If I need help Fernando Claramunt and others can do it much better."

The man shrugged and looked at you with a world-weary expression that seemed to say, These simple foreigners ... "I'll let you know what happens," he ended, turning away.

You walked to the threshold of the dining room. Here you are, you realized, the author of a book whose publication is being celebrated tonight, yet you have nothing to say in the matter. You're an outsider, a foreigner and even worse, an American, an interloper from the New World in this dusky cavern, this Old World where men have been living, fighting and dying for thousands of years. Sure you wrote the book, but the thing that counts most in Spain is to be Spanish, then to have a presence, sway and force of being. More than in any country you know, dominance depends not solely on class, money and might but on the fragile, complex relations between individuals, the web of blood, bonds and friends. Compared to these men, you're powerless, a name, a curiosity: nada. They'd never admit that you might comprehend what's going on here, what's being negotiated right now at that table by the men who have authority, who are on the inside. Although you have forebears from their land, although you've lived and traveled here for decades now, they'll never recognize you as their equal, as one of their own. For them you'll always be a stranger. Accept it, accept yourself. That's how it should be. Your place is on the edge, between this country and your own, where you can see both of them most sharply.

You recalled family dinners long ago when the adult males retired to the living room to smoke and talk business, while the women cleared the table and the children were told to play. Now you've become a little boy again, surrounded by influential men in a restaurant on the other side of the world, almost half a century later. We never cease to be children, gracias a Dios, you thought, smiling. In your mind you perceived the image of your boyhood, the birth of a life that had taken you all the way to where you stood: a young girl running on the sand, pure, free. For a moment you were by the sea again, in the clean sunlight, feeling the wind, breathing the salt air. In the end all our travels, you told yourself, all our journeys might be a search for a spot we already know. Your real life had started in that place and it's still there, by the ocean or on the open roads of Mexico, in the streets of Valencia or Pamplona, in the mountains of León or somewhere else beneath the sky, you saw with a flame of clarity, far more than here in this stuffy, windowless room.

A waiter filled your glass with more Valdepeñas from the barrel. You would have liked to be with Pura and Fernando in the cool alley, but somehow you understood that your spot for now was this stifling, airless space, this battlefield, this bullring—close to the infighting, the horn-butting. You felt isolated, the single non-Spaniard, the one person standing or sitting alone.

The journalist drew up again. "We've struck a deal," he said, keeping an eye on the feud. He hesitated. "But there's a price." The man turned his back to the table and looked at you. He had narrow brown eyes, surrounded by pockets of wrinkles.

"What kind of price?"

"Olano has agreed to leave on condition that you appear on his radio show."

"When?"

"Tonight."

"Tonight? It's already going on eleven o'clock. By the time we have supper and everybody says his piece, it'll be one in the morning."

"You're in Madrid, Señor Estánton," the man replied, giving you a look of patient condescension. "It's a Saturday night during the Feria de San Isidro. Things happen later here than in any other city of Europe, even later during the fiesta. Hombre, it's barely dark outside."

The powwow was breaking up at the table. Your publisher, Federico Ibáñez, all young savvy and confidence, greeted you and took your arm. Leading you to the tavern bar, he said, "Olano is leaving but we have to do our part . . ."

Before Federico could continue, you cut in: "You mean I have to do my part. What if I don't show up at the radio station?"

"*Joder,* you already know about it. That was the condition for getting Olano to leave, Eduardo. We gave him our word—entre hombres, between men. *Qué le vamos a hacer?*" What can we do about it? he asked, shrugging his shoulders in the classic gesture of southern Europe. "Don't worry we're about to enjoy a delicious supper—wild salmon from the País Vasco." He smacked his lips with thumb and forefingers. "This is your night, Eduardo. *Disfrútala,* Enjoy it because our lives are short."

"Nobody consulted me."

Ignoring your comment, Federico said, "Let's go to the banquet room."

As we headed toward the stairway, you felt that you'd been pimped by these grown-up men who were supposed to be looking out for you. We passed Olano and saw him rising to his feet, lifting his body with both hands, making the oak table lurch forward. For a moment his glance crossed with yours. His face was red and pockmarked. He had a nervous tic in both cheeks. Then you noticed that one of his plump, pink hands clutched a copy of your new book, making it appear smaller, like a mouse caught in a lion's paw. You felt a little uneasy about the presentation upstairs—they expected you to give an impromptu speech—but the sight of this man unsettled you much more. He was the troll or minotaur, you were the prey, trapped under a bridge or in a maze, as in some bad dream.

The dining room downstairs at El Callejón is Spain, the banquet room upstairs is Europe. It has none of the somber, earthy atmosphere that makes meals below resemble an archaic ritual. In a word it has no *ambiente,* the subtle balance of space, light, sound and people that a Spaniard can detect unfailingly.

We began the supper with *pisto manchego,* a Castilian ratatouille with colors as bright and varied as the young Goya's palette, followed by salmon steak and a thick, homemade tartar sauce, finished with ice cream and *fresones,* large strawberries from Aranjuez. Spain is still one of the world's last paradises for eating and drinking, you thought, remembering Rodrigo's words on your first trip to Madrid, recalling Botín and the ovens that burn forever. Tonight the food and wine have made everyone forget the clash with Olano. Everyone but you, the scapegoat who must keep the appointment at the station, while they retreat to the bars or to bed.

Over the sobremesa of coffee, brandy and Havana cigars, the introductions and speeches had the long-winded, Latinate, orotund rhetoric of these occasions. You felt grateful to have a book on Hemingway published in Madrid, capital of all the Spains; to have it presented in one of his favorite haunts, especially during San Isidro, when his memory seems most alive. There was a sort of poetic justice to the whole thing that would have made him smile or laugh. But you were too nervous to relax fully, anticipating the radio show with Olano, feeling more like a fall guy than the guest of honor, a naive American who's been *had* once again by older, wiser Europeans—like your friend Rich years ago when Paco cleaned him out in a Madrid boardinghouse.

Somehow the banquet and book-launching are an anticlimax to the real ceremony tonight, you told yourself, the incident and the behind-the-scenes conflict among males with its push-and-shove, tit for tat, give-and-take. That's how it is in Spain: behind the *tienda* there's a *trastienda*, the store behind the store, a word untranslatable into English because it's foreign to our language and to our Anglo-Saxon notions of fair play and openness. So much here remains out of reach, unattainable, like the Armada's gold on the floor of the Irish Sea. Most things can be simpler in America, where we usually know where we stand. In Spain life is often veiled, opaque, with gulfs between what is and what appears to be. "Whatever is not obscure, or chiaroscuro, is not Spanish," one of their writers has said. In spite of progress, free elections, NATO and the European Union, the nation really has not evolved that much into the modern world, you told yourself. Tonight another battle between the old and new Spain has been waged at the Callejón de la Ternera, with words instead of weapons, in a neighborhood defended by loyalists and bombed by fascists in the Civil War.

As the publisher, journalists and critics declaimed in the grandiloquent style affected by Spaniards, you wondered why you felt so unsatisfied, empty. After all, they were saying, this gathering was the fruit of twenty years of travel, study and writing about the country. From their point of view you could be considered a success. Yet it all meant little, their words ringing like gongs in your ears. For some reason you recalled the last scenes of "Citizen Kane," when Orson Welles lies on his deathbed and utters his final word, the name inscribed on the snow-sled of his childhood. All the wealth and splendor of Xanadu mean nothing compared to his memory of the past, the time when he felt himself loved, and his small wooden Rosebud goes up in flames.

So you brought to mind the people and the places that made up your real life in the Spanish-speaking world: Concepción, Lolo, Laura—your teachers; Alfa in Tijuana and all her sisters in Mexico; Gustavo, who led us across the land of our youth; Khedidja, Marga and a few other women in Spain; Alberto, José Mari and Pili, Fernando and Pura sitting at the table with you tonight, the only links between this event and your deeper past, your pursuit, your joy. How lucky you were to find these mentors and companions when you were still young: so many people die without discovering the friends and spaces where they might have become their truest selves, or they find and lose them, or find them too late. The dark sadness of Spain, searing violence of Mexico. Those two countries nourished you, formed and made you what you are, for good or bad. *O México, O España.*

We didn't get off the air until two o'clock at the station. Señor Olano acted like a complete gentleman on the radio, *todo un caballero.* After the long standoff he had gotten his way, exacted his tribute. You had honored your part, completed the ritual, emerged from the labyrinth. Quién sabe, who knows what you said on the program?

When you left the studio in the cool Spanish madrugada, Fernando and Pura were waiting for you at a bar on the corner. We walked to an open-air café to have drinks and listen to musicians playing in the street. By chance they were singing Mexican *boleros* and *rancheras.*

Following the custom of Madrid, we ended the night at dawn in the Puerta del Sol, the city's heart and the eye of Spain. There we drank *chocolate con churros,* hot cocoa thick enough for the sugar-sprinkled fritters to stand by themselves in a cup. Afterwards we walked to the Retiro Park and watched the sun rise over the lake, shimmering on the water, turning it the color of wine.

16. Madrid

Since you were departing that day, the three of us said our good-byes. Those farewells sounded endless, almost in unison, echoing through the years: "Hasta siempre Hasta siempre Hasta siempre..."

Part Four

End of the World

17. Santiago

You needed to get out of the city, out of Madrid, all cities with their grime, noise and strife. You needed to know if you were still free enough to break away, strike out on your own again, leave everything behind for the road.

So you walked on the route traveled by men and women for a thousand years, along a path of stars to Santiago de Compostela and beyond. You followed them to the shrine, toward the setting sun and the ocean, until you could walk no further.

After the clamor of cities you heard the tap of your walking stick on the earth, crunch of gravel underfoot, insects buzzing, birds calling, the bellows of bulls and cows, wind in trees. You entered terrain that has hardly changed in centuries, your feet walking the road as people have walked it for so long. You traveled by day and spent the nights in pilgrims' hospices, in boardinghouses, abandoned schools, ruined churches or under the stars. On clear evenings you could see the Milky Way as you had never seen it before—not a vague cloud but a vast being with trunks, branches, leaves, arms, hands, fingers.

In the mornings the sun rose on perennial scenes: shepherds driving flocks to pasture, men sowing or reaping, women threshing mounds of grain, children splashing in streams. Other sights blotched the pastoral: scraggy dogs and cats, deserted villages with doors batting in the breeze, crumbling walls and hovels. You smelled the warm odors of manure, stables, of bread baking in towns and villages of Navarra, La Rioja, Castilla and León, drank cold, sweet-tasting water from wells, heard cicadas screeching in fields of wheat and rye. Crossing the heartland on foot, you had a sense that you were embracing the whole country, or was it folding you into its tawny, weathered arms?

Rain began to fall as you entered Galicia, the green corner of Spain you had not seen since the first trip more than twenty years ago. It remained the poorest region, where some families subsisted cheek-to-jowl with their cattle, sheep and poultry. Moving forward in space, you seemed to be going backwards in time, in history, into your own past.

If you met other pilgrims, we walked together for a while, mostly in silence, maybe talking a little, all of us keeping our own pace and thoughts, close to one another yet each alone in the rain or mist. We plodded through dripping forests, up and down leafy hills and valleys, our clothes soaking in the soft Galician air. It was as though we were being pushed by a wind at our backs, pulled by a tide, a current of the sea.

Near Compostela we learned the Camino de Santiago had been diverted to make room for an international airport. We felt betrayed by the traffic, the concrete runways and roaring jets, so jarring after the ground we had traveled to arrive this far. Nearby we saw slapdash, gaudy-colored buildings with neon lights flashing at midday, where young women in tight dresses waited outside, laughing and smoking. As though they were errant daughters, as if you were viewing your own story, you regarded them with affection: they recalled an earlier self racked with desire, now worn down by the road, by years and days. The heat, sweat and rain had washed and burned this body, broken it down before making it firm and supple again.

You spotted Compostela from Monte del Gozo—Montjoie, Mount of Joy—as pilgrims have sighted it always. Entering the town, you were returning home to one of the first cities you had seen in Spain, the place where you had discovered the roots of time, the living stone. Moss, weeds and lichen grew from the walls as they did long ago, rain splashed on the shiny, cobbled streets, fog swirled around the domes and towers of churches, palaces, convents.

Full-throated bells guided us to the cathedral. We walked up the wide steps, through the Portal of Glory to a column of grey marble with carved, twined branches and leaves—the tree of Jesse, tree of life. In turn we placed the fingers of our right hand into the five openings, hollowed in stone by the touch of pilgrims countless as stars or grains of sand. The grooves fit smoothly, like a marble glove, still warm from the heat of other hands. Never have you felt more human.

Following the men and women ahead of us, as they followed those before them, we stepped toward the main altar, where we stood in line to embrace the figure of St. James. As a young man you had felt awkward and out of place under his statue. Wrapping your arms around Santiago's broad shoulders now, you were hugging an older friend. You kneeled at the altar, conjuring the people who had aided you on the road and before, praying for them, giving thanks. Your eyes spilled tears, scalding your cheeks and dropping to the age-smoothed stone.

Afterwards you talked with other pilgrims, we strolled through the streets together, greeted new arrivals, ate seafood and drank Ribeiro wine. At midnight we lit a bonfire in the main square, each of us throwing onto the flames a soiled, tattered garment from the journey—a shirt, scarf, a pair of pants or socks. We danced around the fire and said exuberant, watery goodbyes.

From Santiago de Compostela you set out alone again, for Finisterre, Land's End on the last shore of this old world. During three days and nights it rained the rain of Galicia. It fell in the outskirts of the city and in the green hills, the shrouded woods of chestnuts, pines and eucalyptus. It poured on the bridge over the swollen Tambre, where Santiago's disciples are supposed to have fled with his corpse. It showered when you glimpsed the Atlantic through sheets of rain, it was drizzling in the ports with their stale smell of fish and tar, a breeze in your face, and a pale sun falling through clouds that blew over the sea.

When you reached the shore, you crossed a stretch of sand that juts into the ocean, peeled off your clothes and stepped into the surf.

The sun in the west looked like a white wafer through spray and mist. While rain lashed your face, you listened to the wind and waves, the mighty rhythm of the world. You walked into the sea, remembering.

After

This book does not show the good surf at San Onofre, San Clemente, Santa Monica and all the beaches of Alta California with sonorous Spanish names. It does not tell what happened to Tijuana, Ciudad Juárez, Matamoros, Nuevo Laredo or Piedras Negras along the world's most drastic border, the one place where an Anglo-Saxon country stands face to face with the Hispanic world. It does not show how they ravaged those cities, what happened to Alfa and her son Nazario, growing up in old T.J. And what became of Concepción, Lolo, Laura, Zanahorio? *Quihúboles carnales, ¿qué onda, qué onda?*

The book does not have the whales of Baja California, the luminous waters where the desert slides into the sea. Or the oysters in Mulegé, each one a perfect mouthful, so fresh we ate them in the dangerous months, chased with *salsa bandera* the colors of the Mexican flag. It does not tell about lying with second-degree sunburn on damp sheets under a fan in Loreto, and nobody's felt heat unless they've been there in high summer. Or talking with Rosalinda on her balcony in Saltillo, when the world was still young: *"¿Cuándo vienes de nuevo a platicar, Eduardo?"* Watching Popocatépetl veiled in smoke as you stood on the pyramid with Alicia, Alejandro and their boys, the family who helped you know Mexico will abide volcanoes, earthquakes, hurricanes, drugs, its own governments, the United States and more.

There is so much the book did not tell about Spain, the third country that made and nourished you. How you met José Luis and Rosita on the train when they were on their honeymoon, and you jumped off the wooden RENFE carriage in the winter storm at Alcalá de Henares. Where are those snows of yesteryear? How you traveled with Gonzalo in his rattling 2CV, driving roads that led to the whole world—where else could they lead? Or Felipe Arribas stacking cords of wood in Miraflores de la Sierra, before he lay dying like a Spaniard in his own house instead of a hospital, a fire raging in the hearth. Or Germán, the rarest, the wittiest. How could a book have captured him anyway? *Tanta vida, tantísima.*

It does not show the cold, clean-tasting water springing from the well in Hontanas, more blissful than wine, the way it splashed over our hair, our sweated, dirt-streaked faces, our necks and shoulders. How we met Claudio there, a companion for the route or anywhere, the gentlest, wisest. Hasta siempre, *compañero del alma,* siempre.

The book does not have the otherworldly emptiness of Foncebadón, Rabanal del Camino and the villages whose residents have fled to cities in search of jobs, returning only for summer fiestas in honor of their patron saints. The new Spain has not yet killed the old one, but it's trying hard. The nation is still a rope of sand, tugging, fraying at the edges.

It does not tell this or so many things about Spain, all the Spains. It does not show Asturias, Aragón, Extremadura, La Mancha, Andalucía: the passages and whitewashed terraces of Ronda on a summer night when you might be in Africa; drinking sherry and eating serrano ham with Pilar and Antonio Ordóñez at the *finca* that once belonged to his father, the torero who was going to save bullfighting. Who will save it now? And the grave of Orson Welles stood just fifty yards away from us on the shoulder of a winding road.

The book could have told more about Madrid, the city you know better than any other, where you can walk to all the places that count. It could have shown the García Tenorio brothers on Calle de la Bolsa, the best cobblers in the world, who made boots for the kings and queens of Spain, for nobles, politicians, artists, actors, hunters, bullfighters. *"¡Hay que ser más caballero!"* old Carlos and Félix would say, One must be more of a gentleman! And they were the true gentlemen, the finest, los pobres y humildes. And the true damas, the ladies, were also the poor. Where are the damas and caballeros today?

Madrid, whose streets and alleys in the center remind you of a small town, and you can always sense the people. Madrid, *pueblo*. Where the fires never stop burning at Botín. Madrid, where you can see the Sierra de Guadarrama if the smog clears, the mountains where the light changes fast while clouds race across the sky, the peak of Peñalara whose snows used to last through the year.

The book does not have this and so much more about Spain. If you go there and look hard, if you stay for long and go deep enough, you'll find some of it. Maybe the writer's words no longer hold—that it's all changed less than we've grown older. But after your second glass of wine in the long Spanish morning, with sunlight streaming through the windows and fish frying on the grill, it feels nearly the same.

Endnotes

Epigraphs (p. 13): Antonio Machado, "No es el yo fundamental," *Proverbios y cantares* VII; Frank Bidart, "For the AIDS Dead" (2013), *New Yorker* (11 September 2017), pp. 78-79.

Chapter 5. Zanahorio

P. 50: Writer on "the heart of Mexico": Carlos Fuentes, *Una familia lejana* (Barcelona: Bruguera, 1980), p. 180.

P. 51: Theroux on Mexican life as a "vision of battlements": *On the Plain of Snakes: A Mexican Journey* (Boston, New York: Houghton Mifflin, 2019), p. 384. This book is the best and most up-to-date work on contemporary Mexico.

P. 52. Mexican writer on the country's violent topography: Fuentes, *Una familia lejana*, p. 175.

Chapter 7. Castilla

P. 69. Ford on "Bull-fights, bandits, and black eyes": *Gatherings from Spain* (1846; reprint London: J. M. Dent & Sons, 1970), p. 291.

P. 70. Durrell on "two birth-places": *Blue Thirst* (Santa Barbara, CA: Capra Press, 1975), p. 22.

P. 70. León as "capital of winter": phrase coined by the contemporary poet from León, Margarita Merino. See Chapter 15 (Marga).

P. 72. Spanish writer who described the asphyxiating atmosphere of churches: Luis García Montero, *Inquietudes bárbaras* (Barcelona: Anagrama, 2008), p. 155. This and all other translations in the book are mine.

P. 87. Franco as generator of jokes: Gabriel Cardona, *Cuando nos reíamos de miedo: Crónica desenfadada de un régimen que no tenía ni pizca de gracia* (Barcelona: Destino, 2010), p. 46. The following quote by Cardona is from an online interview with RTVE (Radio Televisión Española) on 5 December 2010: http://www.rtve. es/noticias/20101205/francisco-franco-mayor-generador-chistes-historia-espana-segun-gabriel-cardona/381177.shtml

P. 91. "All times past were better": Jorge Manrique, "Coplas por la muerte de su padre" (Verses on the Death of His Father), ca. 1450.

Chapter 8. Cataluña

P. 94. Fish as a religion in Catalonia: Colman Andrews, *Catalan Cuisine: Vivid Flavors from Spain's Mediterranean Coast* (Boston: The Harvard Common Press, 1999), p. 126.

Chapter 9. Khedidja

P. 103. Poet who called the Ramblas the happiest street in the world: Federico García Lorca, in "A las floristas de la Rambla," *Obras completas* (Madrid: Aguilar, 1963), p. 156.

Chapter 11. Botín

P. 134. Tierno Galván's "mayor's banns": Enrique Tierno Galván, *Bandos del Alcalde* (Madrid: Editorial Tecnos, 1986), pp. 35, 50-51.

P. 135. Madrid as "the center of happiness and the joy of Europe": *Los bandos del Alcalde*, p. 111.

Chapter 12. Alberto

P. 150. Poet on the Spain of "*charanga y pandereta*," brass bands and tambourines: Antonio Machado, "El mañana efímero," in *Campos de Castilla* (1912).

Chapter 16. Madrid

P. 233. "... Whatever is not obscure, or claroscuro, is not Spanish": José Bergamín, *Aforismos de la cabeza parlante* (Madrid: Ediciones Turner, 1983), p. 55.

About the Author

Born in Colorado and raised in California, Edward Stanton has lived in Mexico, Argentina, Uruguay and Spain. When the American ministers of hate demonized Mexico and the coronavirus ravaged Spain, he wrote this book as a homage to those countries and their peoples.

Stanton is the author of eleven other books. *Road of Stars to Santiago*, the story of his 500-mile walk on the ancient pilgrimage route to Compostela, was called one of the best works on the subject by the *New York Times*; Pulitzer Prize-winning writer James Michener said of this book, "Edward Stanton recounts his adventures with stylish conviction." Stanton's environmental novel *Wide as the Wind*, the first to treat the tragic history of Easter Island, won the Next Generation Indie Book Award for Young Adult Fiction and three other international prizes. While teaching at colleges and universities in the Americas and Europe, he's also published short stories, poems, translations and essays. The Fulbright Commission, the National Endowment for the Humanities and the Spanish Ministry of Culture have supported his work with grants and fellowships. His students and colleagues recently published *"This Spanish Thing": Essays in Honor of Edward F. Stanton*. At present he's working on a novel set in Argentina after the Dirty War.

Made in the USA
Monee, IL
22 March 2021